MW01616963

'*Pause* is helpful, realis
at once. It is a wonder
do. Full of hope. Thank you, Sarah.'

Carolyn and Christopher Ash, Tyndale House, Cambridge, UK.

'This gem of a book is like sitting down for a refreshing cup of tea with a wise friend. As Sarah walks through some of the challenges that greet women in midlife, she winsomely and compassionately holds out Christ as the one to treasure and trust through it all. It's a book that will grow your understanding and empathy, but most of all, it's a book that will gently lead you to hold onto Christ for yourself, and hold out Christ to others.'

Sarah Dargue, author of *Bumps, Babies and the Gospel* and co-host of *Two Sisters and a Cup of Tea* Podcast.

'I'm so glad Sarah wrote this book! Getting older is not for the faint-hearted and hormonal issues are real, but books on these topics are rare. Sarah gives practical advice saturated in the gospel with plenty of real-life illustrations. She helps us remember that our ultimate hope is not in staying young forever but in an eternity with our Lord and Saviour Jesus Christ.'

Keri Folmar, author of *The Good Portion: Scripture* and co-host of *Priscilla Talk* Podcast.

'You just turned 45! You're feeling trapped and tempted to make choices that will devastate your life. What can you do? *Pause* wisely relates these signs of midlife to a choice we all have – to grow or self-destruct. With humor, transparency, and biblical wisdom, Sarah Allen reveals truth we may never know on our own. God designs a glorious purpose for us in this awkward time of life – to grow!'

Barbara Reaoch, former Director, Bible Study Fellowship International, Children's Division. Author of *A Jesus Christmas* and *A Jesus Easter*.

'Midlife and the menopause are not experiences beyond the transforming power of the gospel. Sarah Allen shows how women can find comfort and joy even in the toughest parts of this phase of life. This is a great read, not only for women but for husbands and pastors to help the women they care about.'

Revd Dr Michael Reeves, President and Professor of Theology, Union School of Theology.

Pause

How to enjoy God,

find hope & bear fruit

through midlife

and the menopause

SARAH
ALLEN

10 Publishing
a division of 10 ofthose.com

Copyright © 2024 by Sarah Allen

The right of Sarah Allen to be identified as the Author of this Work has been asserted by her in accordance with the Copyright, Designs and Patents Act 1988.

British Library Cataloguing in Publication Data
A record for this book is available from the British Library

ISBN: 9781915705327

Designed by Jude May
Cover image © MomentousPhotoVideo | iStock

Printed in Denmark

10Publishing, a division of 10ofthose.com
Unit C, Tomlinson Road, Leyland, PR25 2DY, England
Email: info@10ofthose.com
Website: www.10ofthose.com

1 3 5 7 10 8 6 4 2

*For all my midlife friends
with deep gratitude for your example,
prayers and phone calls.*

Contents

* * *

Introduction

· · ·

My Story

· · ·

A few years ago I found a dress half-price in a sale. The colour was just right, I really liked the style and what a price! I had a wedding coming up and this floral number would be perfect. Once home, I tried it on and it fitted perfectly, slipping smoothly over my figure. Then I glanced in the mirror. Looking back at me was my mother. There were her narrow shoulders and her – how could I put it? – substantial arms. There was the furrow between the eyes and even, could it be possible, a tilt to one side. My dear old mum was almost 80, but in that truth-telling reflection I suddenly saw I was heading fast in the same direction.

No one likes owning up to being middle-aged. No amount of cheery 'Life begins at 40!' or '50 is the new [supply preferred age]' greeting cards can cover up the fact that midlife provides a whole host of challenges. Trying not to look like your mother is the least of them.

When I hit my mid-40s, embarrassing brain fog descended. I not only forgot names, but key words in the middle of meetings. My kids rolled their eyes and thought it was funny. But I wasn't just ashamed, I was actually worried. Could I keep on doing my job when words escaped my mind mid-sentence, and my characteristic forgetfulness ramped up into missing appointments? Were 20 more years teaching English even realistic? Perhaps I should change direction?

Then, just before I turned 50, hot flushes began. Many days I had 15 or maybe 20. My scarf came off, then my cardigan, then I'd quickly put my hair up in a clip, all to relieve the fire that started in my tummy and rose until my face was a tomato. A couple of minutes later back on went the cardigan and the scarf. An hour or so later, it happened all over again. I became an expert in layered dressing. Here was something else for the family to smile at.

Night times were worse, though keeping the window open and having a light-weight duvet helped. Even that would get tossed back a couple of times a night so I could dangle my feet outside the bed, and sometimes I would have to get up to douse myself in cold water. Getting back to sleep after that wasn't always easy. At least my periods had stopped after a few years of not knowing when they would come or how long they would last. Freedom from tampons and sanitary towels, and from cramps and PMT was definitely a blessing, even if the price was a new kind of tiredness.

Time to take control?

For women, ageing is not always gradual and mostly it isn't graceful, as my experience demonstrates. There are times of shock and surprise, and long stretches in which we get used to a new reality, only for it all to change again. The hormones which have kept us aware of time passing each month from puberty onwards, drop off significantly as we hit middle age. Oestrogen levels swing up and down as perimenopause begins and progesterone drops, leading to the menopause – the twelve-month point after the final menstrual period – when both hormones flatline. After this, we're described as post-menopausal, a label which then sticks to the end of our days.

Those medical terms can seem severe, and what they describe might seem scary, but we need to remember that 'the change', as the menopause used to be called, is a regular part of life. My experience is probably typical, but some women barely notice a thing and a significant minority have much more severe symptoms or difficulties which can last for more than a decade. Menopause can be particularly hard to bear when it comes prematurely or suddenly because of medical intervention. It's interesting that the physical and emotional experience also differs culture by culture, though we don't know why that is. But all of us – married or not, mothers or not, career women or not – will be altered in body and mind by these shifts in hormone production.[1]

If you read many of the current, popular books about midlife, you'll notice that they major on serious symptoms and medical treatments. Perimenopause and menopause are hot topics linked as they are to the current cultural conversation on identity and well-being, and they are key issues in a push for true gender equality. The menopause has been called an 'injustice', which needs fixing *now*![2]

Popular titles include Mariella Frostrup's *Cracking the Menopause: While Keeping Yourself Together*.[3] Midlife is a problem to be solved, or even an enemy to be fought. The implication is that a woman's body must be controlled, look great and kept young. As Davina McCall claims on the dust jacket of her best-selling book, *Menopausing*, it's 'time to take control of our bodies and our lives ... This is your body. You owe it to yourself to arm it with the information it needs to navigate this part of your life.'[4]

Taking control and keeping it all together sounds attractive if you're struggling with difficult midlife issues and you'll find these books give out some useful medical information and common-sense advice. Running through most is the proposed solution of Hormone Replacement Therapy (HRT), which replaces the hormones you naturally run out of, reducing symptoms and aspects of female ageing such as decreased bone density.

What these secular books don't do, however, is consider what God has got to do with menopause and midlife. Most don't even discuss how the physical aspects of this stage are related to the work and family changes which often appear around this time. And so, that's what *Pause* is all about. We're going to take some time to step back and think about the bigger picture of female middle age. We'll be asking why we experience this strange stage of life, and how Christian women can live well through it all; family responsibilities, career pressure, ambitions and changing emotions included.

A good starting point

There are many different stages along the journey through midlife. You might be right in the middle of bewildering and painful changes. Alternatively, you could be wondering what all the fuss is about; you're half-way through and doing fine. I'm guessing that quite a few readers will be in their early 40s or even late 30s, curious and perhaps fearful about what is ahead. I hope, too, that there might be some husbands or brothers or pastors who have picked up the book wanting to know how they can help the women they care about.

It's good news then, that Christians, no matter their experience, share a fixed orientation point: the truth that God is good and he is in control. We can say that he is the Lord of all – not just of what seems spiritual – but of our bodies and our moods, our hormones and all our changes. We can confess, with relief, 'all my times are in your hands' (see Ps. 31:15) and know not only that God governs what is going on, but that he cares about it all. The times of loss and the times of gain all belong to him. And his hands which made all the minutes, hours and months, guide our experiences and can redeem them too.

So, throughout *Pause*, I hope you'll see a realism about the problems of midlife, but also real hope that it can be a time of fruitfulness and joy. You'll find God's truth applies to our concerns about ageing looks, regrets over the past, the demands to care for others and our fears for the future. And together we'll explore the temptations we face to check-out spiritually, judge others and follow idols of comfort.

Trying to make time stand still or our bodies stop changing is foolish. But pausing to understand how God's eternal wisdom relates to our changing seasons is invaluable for navigating the hard yards of our middle years. When we take a step back to think biblically, God's Spirit can lead us to enjoy a greater security in our faith, peace in our identity and usefulness in our ever-changing world.

Chapter 1

* * *

What's the Problem with Time Passing?

* * *

Understanding why change hurts

Rachel runs her life with a minutely calibrated schedule, timetables stuck to her fridge and a watch that pings incessantly with reminders and alarms. Her job in the health service, church involvement and large family (a five-year-old as well as three teenagers) mean that home life, from folding the laundry to phone calls with her mum, must work by the clock. Her discipline is genuinely impressive, but even that can't guarantee productivity. Stuff happens. Frustration very often rules. Today, the train was delayed, and she missed a meeting. Then, as she rushed to the supermarket, her period arrived. Work trousers spoilt, she had to go home to change – and with no food for tea.

Rachel feels very keenly that time is passing moment by moment, and that she's running to keep up, often literally. And it's not only long to do lists causing this pressure; her body and brain are changing, making it harder to go at the pace she used to. She's 45 and her previously predictable periods have gone haywire: her bleeding is heavier and she never quite knows when they'll come. She should go to the doctor, but that's more disruption and more time away from tasks.

Rachel's also becoming conscious that time is passing in a different way. These changes in her body seem to have caught her unaware. She's not only losing minutes when things go wrong, she feels she's losing her identity as she moves forwards into another stage of life. She feels the same inside as she did at 25, or just about, and yet now she can't get by without reading glasses and running for the bus leaves her knee joints protesting. Time seems to be taking the old Rachel away.

Time plays tricks

Think about the way we talk about time in English. We buy a new device so that we can '*save* time', we decide to '*invest* time' in people or projects, and sometimes we confess guiltily that we have '*wasted* time'. You might even make decisions on how to '*spend* time' by reflecting that 'time *is money*'. In all these expressions, time is a precious commodity, a limited resource, which belongs to us and is for us to conserve or use as we see fit.

Yet, as Rachel is experiencing, and as we have always known deep down, time is something we can never quite keep hold of. If our moments should be conserved or only spent wisely, then it's no wonder we feel great disappointment when we see them ticking away, the evidence etched on our faces and marked in our bodily cycles. And for those who live by the clock, like Rachel, our powerlessness to stop or slow down its moving minutes can even make us panic.

Many of us get to midlife and say to ourselves: How on earth did *that* happen? The answer is obvious: time passes and so we age. But the experience of living in time doesn't quite fit with the neatly marked days and weeks on the calendars. Time doesn't seem to progress steadily or feel measured at all. In one season, time stands still, then in another it rushes on crazily, and while we're engrossed in the present moment, the future is upon us. Virginia Woolf described this very vividly at the beginning of the last century:

Why, if one wants to compare life to anything, one must liken it to being blown through the Tube [the London Underground] at fifty miles an hour, landing at the other end without a single hairpin in one's hair! Shot out at the feet of God entirely naked! ... With one's hair flying back like the tail of a race-horse. Yes, that seems to express the rapidity of life, the perpetual waste and repair; all so casual, all so haphazard.[1]

We may feel foolish for being surprised when we see lines on our faces, after all, we know logically we should expect them. But like Virginia Woolf's character here, we can feel powerless and even 'naked' in the face of such a blind force and the apparently chaotic rush of life.

God makes time

The hard truth is that time doesn't belong to us at all. It has never been a human possession. In Colossians 1:16, Paul makes it clear that all time is Christ's. We learn that 'in him all things were created: things in heaven and on earth, visible and invisible, whether thrones or powers or rulers or authorities'. Time, that invisible, powerful force, was created by him.

Remember back in Genesis 1, as God makes light; he calls the light 'day' and the darkness 'night'. That's Christ, the Word of God, making time. And when we read Jesus 'is before all things' (Col. 1:17), Paul's telling us not only that Christ existed before creation (which of course he did), but also that he is beyond it. Theologians have described God as being in 'the now that stands still', an eternal present, totally apart from our kind of time. And because he is beyond, or above, our ever-passing time, he is able to rule over it.

This means that, rather than time blowing us along in a 'casual, haphazard' manner, Christ is ordering time. He holds the reins of the minutes and the hours because 'in him all things hold together' (Col. 1:17). He makes sure that time doesn't run away or slow down to nothing; time is steady in his good hands and moves forwards 'for him' (Col. 1:16).

So, though Rachel feels as if time is playing unkind tricks on her, furrowing lines in her forehead and upending her regular cycles, she can remember that time is not in charge, Christ is. God is working out his great and good purposes in time in every tick of the clock and turn of the calendar page.

Back in Genesis 1, we get a glimpse of what God's purposes are. Through Jesus, he establishes a world not only separated into different spaces but also structured in terms of time. Created on the fourth day, the sun, moon and stars 'serve as signs to mark sacred times, and days and years' (Gen. 1:14). All living things are bound into these cycles of day and night, weeks, months and years. In the rhythms of his time, trees 'bear fruit' (Gen. 1:11) and birds 'increase in number' (Gen. 1:22), while humanity is called to 'be fruitful and increase in number; [to] fill the earth and subdue it' (Gen. 1:28).

So time is not a mechanical force, still less a trickster. Its regular rhythms are created by the good, personal God and experienced in the minds, bodies and souls of the people he has made. Still, we're not totally off the mark when we think of time as a precious resource, nor are we wrong to connect time to productivity. Time is God's gift for the joyous multiplication and cultivation of all good things. And all this abundant increase is for one even greater purpose: Christ's own glory.

Dust, decay and death

The problem is, of course, that we live in a world where that desire and call to be productive has been blighted. Romans tells us that creation has been 'subjected to frustration' (Rom. 8:20), and this is something we taste every day, just ask Rachel. It's true that God is in charge of time, but it is also true that life is haphazard. Things go awry, they wear out and break down. Our bodies don't just follow good and easy patterns. Periods are painful; fibroids, endometriosis and polycystic ovaries disrupt our hopes; PMS and perimenopause, hot flushes and vaginal atrophy exhaust and embarrass us. Time passing, whether in natural, regular cycles, or disordered ones, sometimes seems to lead to fruitlessness, not abundance.

Genesis tells us that unlike the animals we – both men and women – are made in God's likeness and image (Gen. 1:26–27). The first people were made to be like the one who is outside of time, shining out his glory in the world. Yet they are also made in time, out of the dust of the earth (Gen. 2:7). From the very start, humanity both stems from a royal line, and is as common as muck; living in time and made for immortality. And because Adam and Eve are made by God, they belong to him and he delights in them. But you know the story: this perfect couple messes up. They listen to a voice of deceit, and they disobey the truth-speaking God. And so they 'return to the ground' (Gen. 3:19); they cannot 'live for ever' (Gen. 3:22).

God dictates that humanity will have broken relationships and that women will endure agony in childbearing (Gen. 3:16). The trials of menopause, as well as other gynaecological troubles can be seen as part of this specific cursing of women's fertility. It's no wonder that periods can be painful, and the loss of them is sometimes brutal too.

Men are also blighted: they experience ongoing struggle in their work to make the ground fertile (Gen. 3:17–18). The multiplication and cultivation commanded at the very beginning continues, but it is limited and corrupted through our rejection of God. Middle age, and all it entails for both men and women, involves not just feeling our limitations, but experiencing decay, the returning to dust pronounced on Adam and Eve.

Dylan Thomas, an atheist, wrote a poem for his father which responds to this sense of imminent decay. Expressing the hunger for life here and now, he urges his father:

Do not go gentle into that good night
... Rage, rage against the dying of the light.[2]

We want to cling to youth and fight against our mortality, despite the fact that death has been our lot since the day Adam and Eve lost the garden. And many of us want to rage against midlife and menopause too, feeling that this change and pain is unfair and should be fought. We don't want to go gently into our 50s or 60s at all.

Pausing to remember the origin of our decay and our hormonal trouble helps us here. They are not simply natural processes which we should glide through smiling, but neither should we shake our fists at their unfairness and fight tooth and nail against them. The struggles of menopause remind us forcefully that this world is broken; it is under God's judgement and needs his grace. It shows us that our bodies, just like time itself, are not actually our own creations or under our control. We need our Maker's help.

Changing time

I'm writing this in the season of Advent. Lights are coming on in our street and I'm feeling pressure to get the decorations up and presents bought. As schmaltzy music blares out of the shops, it's easy to be taken in by all the bling and the hurry, and forget that Christmas centres on the infinite God 'being made in human likeness' (Phil. 2:7) and entering time.

And the second person of the Trinity didn't just step into time. As man, he grew and changed in time. He had nine months developing in Mary's womb, then birth and suckling, then weaning, teething and toddling. He celebrated the annual festivals with his family, grew out of his clothes and hit puberty.

Jesus 'grew in wisdom and stature, and in favour with God and man' (Lk. 2:52). He experienced how time changes bodies and relationships. And along the way, all the way to the cross, he experienced the difficulties of change and physical pain, just as we do. Of course, he didn't go through the menopause or live into middle age, but what Jesus did suffer means that he is fully able to sympathise with us in our weakness (Heb. 4:15).

God is eternally compassionate, and now Christ's sufferings make him a High Priest, who – we can be sure – truly represents us and truly understands us. In the trials of midlife, when we are flummoxed or frustrated, we can pause and call out to the one who promises to 'help us in our time of need' (Heb. 4:16).

But it isn't just sympathy we see as Christ entered our human struggle, or even a better kind of divine help. He came to die. And the aid he offers us as High Priest comes only through his death. Like the animal whose skin covered the shame of Adam and Eve (Gen. 3:21), Christ's life was sacrificed so that the sin of all who trust in him would be covered. In place of their shame would be his perfection. In place of their curse is his peace (Col. 1:20).

By being the long-anticipated substitute, bearing the wrath of God against our rebellion, Jesus mended the cause of time's disorder, that fractured relationship between sinful man and a holy God. Rising from the grave and then ascending into heaven, he showed us that death's power has been broken. Decay and dust are not the end.

Of course we still live in the era of the 'haphazard' and 'perpetual waste and repair' Virginia Woolf describes; our middle-aged lives are messy, and the changes of menopause feel a lot like waste. But that's less than half of the Christian's reality. A new resurrection age has been inaugurated. Midlife is another stepping stone on the Christian's journey towards that new life with Christ, where there will be 'no more death or mourning or crying or pain, for the old order of things has passed away' (Rev. 21:4).

You may be decaying but you are already clothed in his beauty, and each passing day takes you closer to this eternal reality which 'can never perish, spoil or fade ... kept in heaven for you' (1 Pt. 1:4). Even now, in our weight gain, greying hair and disrupted sleep, we have Christ in us, 'the hope of glory' (Col. 1:27).

Looking ahead

Rachel's menopause and midlife story has barely started. She's got quite a few years of managing symptoms ahead – however mild or difficult they turn out to be – alongside her busy work and family life. She knows it will continue to be a challenge, but she's holding on to her hope in the gospel of renewal. The physical change she's starting to experience will not be wasted. She's already being forced to cry out to God more, as she finds her plans are often upended, and she's also actually looking forward to where he's taking her.

A period-free life with no chance of pregnancy any longer sounds a very good deal for a start, conscious though that this is a great grief to some, including her childless sister-in-law. But she reckons there's still a glimpse of God's kindness in this timing. Who would want to be managing a baby in their 60s or PMS in their 80s? It was hard enough having an unexpected baby when she was 40! And the movement away from the menstrual cycle will be a break that gives a tiny foretaste of things to come in the new creation, when the curse is fully dealt with and there's no more marriage or procreation. On that day, there will be no more pain and all our hopes will be satisfied in Christ.

But midlife doesn't mean an end to multiplication and cultivation, of course. The task of bringing order, beauty and life goes on, in new ways. Reading the Bible before she fell asleep that exhausting day of the missed meeting and failed supermarket shop, Rachel saw something fresh in Jesus' familiar words in Matthew 28:18–20:

> *All authority in heaven and on earth has been given to me. Therefore go and make disciples of all nations, baptising them in the name of the Father and of the Son and of the Holy Spirit, and teaching them to obey everything I have commanded you. And surely I am with you always, to the very end of the age.*

While she was still feeling annoyed by her lack of control over the timings of her day – from the train to her heavy period – she was hit by the reality of Jesus' authority and presence. In that seeming disorder, he was with her, because she is part of his people. Her schedule quite obviously hadn't ruled the day, but Jesus' plan had. All her best efforts to be productive and cram in what her four kids needed and what her husband needed and what her colleagues needed, to make things right and nice for them all, had, at best, mediocre results. She breathed out some of the tension she held in her shoulders with a smile.

To the end of this age, in her ever-changing life, he was with her and his command to live fruitfully wasn't all about getting her stuff done well, or about being 'on top of things', or even about making sure everyone else was okay. There was a greater purpose in view. The ruling and multiplying had been reshaped by the new mandate to make disciples and, along with them, to obey his commands. To trust, to love, to follow. That was it.

Rachel fell asleep quickly that night. She was shattered after all. And the next day she blinked awake to her alarm, and to the next lot of lists and reminders. Life wasn't any different. But she remembered that she was living in God's time, in the age ruled by Christ, and he was with her by his Spirit. He was ordering the patterns of her life, her regular heartbeats and rather erratic hormones, the going out of the house in the morning and the school pick-ups in the afternoon. She knew that this day her own plans would end up changing and there would, no doubt, be moments of disorder and frustration, but as she worked to get her tasks done, Jesus was building his kingdom. And somehow, as she ticked things off her list, and trusted, loved and followed, he would be doing it through her.

Reflection:

1. Where are you in your midlife journey? How are you currently experiencing the frustration of this fallen world in your everyday life?

2. The book of Revelation provides us with a picture of Christ in glory looking like a lamb who has been slain. What does the fact that our ruling Lord entered into mortal time and suffered to conquer death tell you about what he is like?

3. Meditate on this verse today:

   But I trust in you, LORD;
   I say, 'You are my God.'
   My times are in your hands ... (Ps. 31:14–15)

   How might these truths bring you comfort when you feel that change and disorder are overwhelming?

Chapter 2

* * *

What If?

* * *

Dealing with regret and loss

Melanie struggles to sleep at night. She flops into bed exhausted, but wakes in the early hours hot and sweaty, and that's when her thoughts begin to spiral, keeping her awake for an hour or two. Round and round goes the question: What if I hadn't decided to go into mission work in my 20s?

Maybe then I'd have been able to get a proper career, she thinks, and have a decent pension waiting for me. If I hadn't gone overseas, then I wouldn't be stuck with short-term posts and low-paid work.

Melanie is right. The window for getting established in a profession closed a long time ago. That exciting opportunity abroad had seemed right at the time but now, 20 years later, Melanie feels dissatisfied and regretful. And it's not just what she came back to that's hard to take. The mission she'd begun with such enthusiasm turned out to be marred by difficult relationships and disappointments. The leadership had not only been poor, but key individuals had shown themselves to be immature and self-interested. The whole experience has left her feeling shaken in her faith and cynical about Christian work even after all these years. If only I had taken more advice, or if leaders had actually behaved as they should, she tells herself, I wouldn't be in this situation now.

Melanie's situation may be very different from yours, but it's unlikely you've got to middle age without experiencing some form of regret over a past choice. It could be centred on a relationship road not taken or mistakes you feel you've made with your children. The grief might be related to parents or siblings, or perhaps friendships lost along the way. There might be one incident – the time you lost your temper in public or that occasion you failed to speak out – which you replay again, and again, and again. These 'what-ifs' and 'if-onlys' act like a pebble in your shoe producing a familiar, persistent pain. As regret fosters both blame and sorrow, you limp onwards, slowed down by the discomfort, and hardened towards others and towards God.

Looking at what is lost

Regret, of course, can be experienced at any point in life, but as we hit a mid-way point it's natural to start looking back. And looking back can lead to emotions which take us by surprise. The physical changes of menopause themselves can trigger real questions and sadness about what has been lost. As Melanie has found, the opportunities and choices of youth are long gone, having left along with the wrinkle-free skin and super-supple joints she now realises she took for granted. She laments her losses and asks why they had to be so hard. Nothing she can do will give her back the options she had before she went on the mission field, just as no medication will reverse the effects of ageing in her body.

And as much as the prospect of no more periods might bring relief for some, approaching the end of fertile years is often a time of grief. Some women moving into their mid-40s might long for more children but realise that this is less and less likely. Coming to terms with the end of a certain stage of mothering can be hard, too. Kids approaching adulthood increasingly make their own way in life and appear to need us less, sometimes going in a direction which wrenches our hearts. For those like Melanie who haven't had children, this finality may be yet more painful, and fears arise of a future without the practical care and companionship of descendants. Memories of relationships not pursued, delayed or broken, in the light of this grief can be very bitter indeed.

Coupled with this sadness, a drop in hormones beginning in perimenopause often brings on mood changes which can make it more difficult to process our regrets well. The next chapter will focus on feelings more closely, but it's worth reflecting on how our natural tendency to look back at this stage of life can become hazardous for those experiencing an upsurge in unfamiliar emotions. Irritability, anger and sadness can make us look back more, and make it harder to see the past or the present in a clear light.

Clear your vision

Our dog is dangerously attracted to cats. Walking around the neighbourhood he is on tenterhooks, straining at the lead as he goes past houses where he remembers cats hang out. And there have been a couple of occasions when this obsession has got him into trouble. He's been so gripped by sighting a cat that he's run straight into a lamppost. Looking over his shoulder at a lost opportunity, has meant he's missed the present obstacle and ended up with a very sore head.

A dog getting distracted can be comic. Less amusing is when we're so wrapped up in the past that we run into present danger. And that's where Melanie has got to. She can feel the risk of regret hardening her heart, her thoughts stuck and her hope for the future drying up. She knows she needs help in changing the way she views the years gone by.

So, what should Melanie do? And what should we do when our what-ifs and if-onlys threaten to damage our present? The few secular books on midlife mentioning this type of re-evaluation offer a brisk remedy: Life is short and if you don't like something, then change it. Forget the past and move on. Live for now. But such advice isn't always best: there are things Melanie can't change, and sometimes there are things which we shouldn't change. What's more, our best attempts to move on can be overshadowed by the very memories we're trying hard to leave behind.[1] We need more than a pep talk.

Perhaps the first thing is to remember who we are. We're not God. He knows all the stars in the sky, the hairs on our head and the end from the beginning (Is. 40:26, 46:10; Mt. 10:30). We know very little. We're people of limited minds and restricted vision. There's always far more complexity in the past than we can grasp; when we look back, our memories are not complete. Melanie remembers the way the team leader let her down, but not her own failure to take responsibility. She dwells on the career opportunities lost, but she can't know if they would actually have led to a job she would have enjoyed.

Rather than getting stuck in a muddle of blame and responsibility, it is better for Melanie to rest in an acknowl-edgment of her limited, childlike knowledge. This is not defeatism or weakness but true, God-honouring humility. As we apply these truths to our own situations, there may well be a need to try and sort through very painful memories, perhaps with a trusted friend or a counsellor, particularly if they centre on serious harm done to us. But whatever the scale of our past regrets and hurts, we can only begin to clear our vision when we see that only God has the full picture.

This doesn't however mean that the secular advice of 'forget the past, live for now' is correct. The Bible commands a different approach. Looking back *is* encouraged, but it isn't the kind that results in a collision with a lamppost, knocking us in distress, and making us unable to act well in the present. God tells us to look back so we can face our regrets, and to do that well, we need to look beyond our own brief lives. We need to go further back, back into salvation history.

Look to the cross

If Melanie's struggle is with choices she regrets and frustration over the inadequacies of others, her long-time friend Anna wrestles with her own failings. They began to talk about this over coffee one day. Both of them looked shattered, and Anna reluctantly explained what was keeping her awake. Melanie has known Anna's two boys since they were babies, and heard Anna's stories of their ups and downs over the years. Now in their 20s, neither of them is a Christian, and one of them has mental health problems. This time Anna confided that it wasn't just heartache over their unbelief and struggles that kept her from falling asleep. It was her sense of responsibility.

Could it be that her short temper has made them turn away from God? Was her strictness the reason why her youngest battles depression? She knows that often she lashed out with her tongue when she should have over-looked his childish mistakes. Even as she recounts her questions to Melanie, Anna berates herself; 'I've failed as a mum,' she says, 'I can't believe that I was such a bad parent, I remember when…'

As she returns to the past again and again, reliving the arguments and her angry outbursts, there is only one thing that can interrupt her thought-cycles of blame, and that is looking back to the cross. Acknowledging that God knows all, and her view is limited, she comes to a striking conclusion. Her lack of self-control was even worse than she remembers. It deserves death under God's right judgement. Christ died for her wounding words and unwise discipline. It's almost unbearable to reflect on, but the consequences of her sin that her sons tasted fell even harder on Jesus. As it fell, though, the price was paid. The agony ended and Christ said, 'It is finished' (Jn. 19:30). Anna – and you and I, too – need to believe him.

In Colossians – a book we will return to throughout *Pause* – Christ is presented to us as a reconciling ruler. He's a King who is in the business of 'making peace' for he has worked cosmically to 'reconcile to himself all things, whether things on earth or things in heaven' (Col. 1:20). While we don't see this monumental peace right now, we do see people turned from enemies at odds with God and in thrall to a dark enemy, rescued to become subjects of his kingdom of light. And we are those people if we are trusting in his name. Paul says that being made at peace with God, we are 'holy in his sight, without blemish and free from accusation' (Col. 1:22). These words soothe when our minds are spinning in circles. The holy God sees us as spotless; blame is over.

Remembering forgiveness

And there is more; Christ rose. Anna knows that his death led not just to a wiping away of sin, but also a provision of new, holy life. This forgiveness covers not only the sins of child- and teenager-hood, but also the sins committed while being a Sunday-school-teaching, trying-to-do-her-best, continuing-in-her-faith Christian mum. God still calls her 'blameless' and 'holy', so, to honour him, she must live in a daily remembrance of his forgiveness and not keep on accusing herself.

And that's so often what regret is: a shame-filled self-accusation. We fill our minds with recriminations when we deal with 'what-ifs' and 'if-onlys', showing that we struggle to accept Christ's rule and his grace. We may admit we are blemish free in God's eyes, but when we look back, all we can see is the stain. Perhaps we even say out loud, 'I know I am forgiven, but I can't forgive myself.'

Underneath this humble-sounding claim there lurks the idea that 'I thought I was better than that.' It's hard to acknowledge that the 'mistakes' we made were not due to the time of the month, or other people, or menopausal brain fog (though these certainly have played a part) but because deep down our hearts are twisted by sin. We won't *feel forgiven* if we refuse to accept how desperately *we need forgiveness*. And yet there is real peace when we confess our sins and say, as the late Tim Keller famously and frequently said, 'We are [– I am! –] more sinful and flawed in ourselves than we ever dared believe, yet at the very same time we are more loved and accepted in Jesus Christ than we ever dared hope.'[2]

What we need to do, then, is let go of the memories we're clutching like comfort-toys and grab hold of the gospel. This means breaking those well-worn habits and routines; getting out of bed to pick up a Christian book when we're tempted to keep churning things over late at night, for example, or putting on a worship song when we're driving and prone to mull over the past. It might mean asking a friend to pray very specifically that we'd have strength to turn away from the memories or thoughts that plague us. Whatever the strategy, it all serves this need: to 'continue in [our] faith, established and firm, and … not move from the hope held out in the gospel' (Col. 1:23). We will only know we are safe, forgiven and holy, as we keep fixed on to Christ.

Applying forgiveness

If embracing God's forgiveness enables us to look at our past mistakes without disabling regret, it also helps us to deal with the past failings of others. Part of Melanie's frustration comes from the bad behaviour of those she had looked up to.

When Melanie thinks about the situation she feels anger rising. There had been leaders on the mission whose administration was inadequate and one in particular who seemed more interested in winning applause than Christ-like service. Though it was over 20 years ago, she regrets her decision to join the team and she resents the sin of those who made it so hard. But if Melanie wants to know the joy of the forgiveness she's received, then God's Word insists she must forgive those who sinned against her (Col. 3:13; Mt. 6:9–15).

It works like this: if I am a sinner who has received such forgiveness at such an incredible price, who am I to cling on to lists of the flaws and crimes of others? I can acknowledge these sins honestly, as I acknowledge my own. Forgiving others takes time; it isn't a one-off event, but a repeated, persistent and often painful choice to let go of or better, to give up anger and resentment.

Some of us who've been seriously sinned against will benefit from talking this through with a pastor, wise friend or counsellor. As you seek to forgive, you may want to speak honestly to the one who has hurt you, expressing forgiveness and seeking a way of reconciliation. But whether this is a route you can take or not, forgiveness is a handing over the right to vengeance and trusting that person to God. I can leave my regrets, my sins and the one who has sinned against me in the hands of the all-just, all-wise, all-merciful Lord.

Looking back to see the future

If God were not ordering 'all things' for the glory of Jesus, if things were out of his control, Melanie would be right to weep herself into weary and bitter resignation to the frustrations of her life. But she knows God, and is beginning to see how his cosmic plan 'to reconcile to himself all things' (Col. 1:20) encompasses even the details of her muddled life. The story isn't over, and the ending will be glorious.

This knowledge enables us to bring the pain of past disappointments to him. We cry out to him in lament, telling our Father about the unloveliness and cruelty of life precisely because we know that he is loving and just. We cry out because we don't see that love and justice displayed as we feel it should be, or as we know it will be one day. We cry out because we are safe in those loving arms, as an injured child sobs when her mum picks her up from the floor, knowing in relief that her mum understands, and cares, and listens, and that it will all be all right in the end.

In Colossians, Paul describes the 'gospel' as if it were a gigantic, leafy vine, with many fertile shoots. It is bearing fruit 'throughout the whole world' (Col. 1:6) and this happens as Christians in their local churches, like the one in Colossae, believe the good news about Jesus and '[bear] fruit in every good work' (Col. 1:10). Whatever the individual circumstances – past mistakes and present regrets – of these ancient Christians' lives, Paul is confident that they are part of God's fruitful work and building towards a glorious eternity.

As I write this chapter, I'm looking out onto my garden and the three pear trees planted as weak saplings by the previous owners of our house. They have survived winter frosts, torrential Yorkshire rain and a few very dry summers, as well as plenty of poor pruning on my part. They don't look much, but for the last few years they have produced abundant crops. Despite the seeming battle against all the odds, these pear trees are simply doing what they were planted for.

In the same way, along with those Christians 2,000 years ago, if we are believing in Christ, then we are part of his orchard. And with the all-powerful God as the gardener, the fruit of people becoming Christians, and the fruit of lives looking more and more loving and patient and joyful will keep on coming. This kind of fruitfulness is what we have been saved for. His priority for us isn't projects completed or careers peaking, but a trust in Christ which transforms us into his likeness.

We may deeply grieve foolish diversions from what was wise, and even more, the way we have consciously chosen sin. Our hearts will ache in agony over the loss of employment, or loved ones, or the family we'd dreamed of. God's pruning sometimes cuts sharp and deep, but we mustn't think that he takes pleasure in pain or that he just wants to shock us into action. Rather, the seeming randomness of 'time and chance' which affects everyone on this earth (Ecc. 9:11), the joys as well as the losses, if now we are securely rooted in Christ, will result in rich fruitfulness.

Our plans fail, and we fail, but God's purposes have never failed and will never fail. Paul Tripp nails it when he writes, 'life never works to our plan because our individual stories are all part of a greater story. The central character of the STORY is sovereign over each detail of our stories'.[3] In other words, as Paul tells the Colossians, Christ 'is before all things, and in him all things hold together'. All things are arranged so that 'in everything he might have the supremacy' (Col. 1:17–18). Christ's rule is primary and total and glorious. His story is far better than any we could have written for ourselves.

So, when Melanie wakes at night, regretting her decision to do mission work, she can turn her mind to this better story. Considering God's overarching plan helps her to look for the shoots and buds of grace. She remembers one woman who professed faith despite her family opposing her decision to follow Christ. Perhaps the Lord used that frail beginning and perhaps there's now fruit among her relatives Melanie knows nothing of? Then there was a small Bible study which sprang up. Maybe those young Christians grew in faith, despite the squabbles she witnessed?

Whatever the problems which blighted the project, and despite the limitations it brought to her career, Melanie can rest in the knowledge that in everything Jesus was ruling, and fruit was being formed. And she can trust, as well, that in her life today he is ruling, and still has plans for a good harvest.

Reflection:

1. What memories do you return to which feed regret or blame? Consider how the Lord has already, or might now, use this memory to grow your faith or that of others.

2. Who do you need to forgive? Do you need to be reassured God has forgiven you? Read Luke 23:26–56 slowly, noticing all the different characters around the cross and how Jesus treated them. Pause to meditate with gratitude on the richness of his forgiveness shown to the guilty, both those who harmed him and his followers who betrayed him.

Chapter 3

⁕ ⁕ ⁕

Who Can Help Their Moods?

⁕ ⁕ ⁕

Finding a way through distress

Sasha looked in the mirror one day and didn't recognise herself. It wasn't the changes in her skin that disturbed her, but the tense expression on her face. Who had she become? Her emotions had been all over the place for the previous few months: she cried every day, flew off the handle at her teenage daughters and felt overwhelming panic when she looked at the state of her house. The person in the mirror wasn't the all-competent nurse she used to be, instead she saw someone not coping at all.

Anxiety and frustration seemed to have taken up permanent residence in Sasha's life whereas previously she'd only ever experienced them as fleeting feelings. Her family noticed how low she was and Sasha felt as though they were tiptoeing round her, trying not to cause upset, whether tears or fury. In that scary moment before the bathroom mirror, she found herself wondering whether everyone would be better off without her.

Changes to mood are a key symptom of perimenopause and menopause. And within this, a central experience seems to be what one medical journal calls, 'anger, irritability, or tendency towards conflict'.[1] This shouldn't be a surprise; we all know that hormones affect the way we feel about life, whether those distant yo-yo-ing teenage moods or much more recent struggles with the monthly dips of PMS that the majority of women go through, some to an extreme degree.[2] It's no wonder, then, that at least 20 per cent of women report heightened mood difficulties in perimenopause, some going through the profound distress that Sasha faces.

For many of us, 'brain fog' – forgetting things and not being able to concentrate or think as clearly as we previously did – makes matters worse. I've been teaching English since my 20s but I remember standing at the board in my classroom a few years ago, pen poised. I had written an 'o' with my pen, but the term I needed vanished from my head, and I blushed, stuttered and dried up. It wasn't that I couldn't spell the troublesome word, it was that I couldn't locate it. I was terrified. In all my years of teaching poetry nothing like this had ever happened before. Was I going mad? Had I early-onset dementia? How could I do my job if I couldn't remember the basics?

It was some kind of relief to find out that many women far more proficient than me go through exactly the same panic. The high-flying lawyer and politician Baroness Warsi speaks about how she sometimes found herself in media interviews and 'lost the ability to construct sentences'.[3] From someone who prided herself on being able to think quickly on her feet, her confidence faltered, and she became someone dependent on detailed planning. She confesses, 'I was starting to lose part of me.'[4]

The Triple-H-Threat

Baroness Warsi is just one of the many contributors to Kaye Adams and Vicky Allan's book *Still Hot!*, a collection of real-life menopause stories. The majority of women who relate their experiences there, whether of life-changing anxiety, depression or significant problems with memory, were also carrying the substantial weights of grief, work pressure and family issues, often all at once. It's as if in midlife, women face a perfect storm of stressors; what I call a Triple-H-Threat to their sense of self.

Hormones

It's not hard to see how hormonal changes which usually begin in our 40s can bring difficult moods. Writer Keri Folmar describes hormones as like a spoon plunged into the soup of our lives, stirring things up.[5] Anger, anxiety and deep sadness can emerge when our hormones intermittently or increasingly disturb what has been lying low. What we've managed successfully before, or simply ignored, is no longer manageable. When sleep is broken by night sweats and we feel upset by a sudden onset of forgetfulness or when extremely heavy and erratic periods mean we are exhausted, the emotional disturbances hormones cause can become even more unbearable.

On an in-patient psychiatric unit near me we see the evidence. Nancy, an occupational therapist, told me about the spread of ages on her all-female ward; there are young adults who are struggling, dementia patients, and a significant number of perimenopausal and menopausal women. It's not that a drop in oestrogen is the sole cause of mental ill health in this age group, but it can stir up a previously well-managed condition or sometimes play a part in a new period of mental ill health. Yet, Nancy's patients are not just experiencing hormonal shifts and brain-chemistry problems, they are coping with midlife *life* problems, as well.[6]

While many of the current media activists see hormonal imbalance as the key problem for middle-aged women, and access to HRT as an issue of women's rights, other life difficulties are often left unaddressed. But hormones are only one element of the Triple-H-Threat to our midlife moods, and medication can only be part of an answer to the problems we might encounter.

Habitat

Alongside the very real difficulties of hormonal disturbances, the second element of threat for some (though certainly not for all) is the situation, or the habitat, we dwell in.

Where you live, your family environment and your work situation all impact your sense of self.

In midlife, each of these can become especially stressful. There's being squeezed between the demands of ageing parents and dependent children (possibly with teenagers going through their own hormonal battles like Sasha) or perhaps dealing with the loss of parents or a new kind of grief as fertile years come to an end. Add to this complex schedules, the ins and outs of running a home, and the pressures of paying the bills, and things quickly feel stretched.

Having been of working age for around 20 years, with possibly another 20 to go, we can be facing significant career pressures, too – not least the troubling question of whether we are doing the right thing in the right place. Things rarely feel as sorted as we wish they were. By the age of 40, we perhaps expect to have everything sorted – a nice house, a nice family, nice work situation – so when middle age doesn't deliver these, and instead presents us with real complications, the strain can be hard to manage.

Hurt

The final threat which is often stirred into this dangerous mix is hurt. Half-way through life, we've likely experienced all manner of ups and downs as we looked at in the previous chapter; at the least we'll have been let down by others, at the worst, we've been abused. We might seem competent on the outside, but underneath, painful wounds may well remain. The bullies at high school, parental putdowns, bereavements, a broken marriage, the abortion you were pressured into. All of these can be significant factors in the mood swings we experience.

Before we move on to practical steps to help to manage moods when faced with this Triple-H-Threat, there's another H to consider. When it comes to moods, our hearts are the final piece of the puzzle.

The heart of the matter

Lucy is in perimenopause and just recently has begun to have night sweats once or twice each night. She wakes up blazing hot in sweaty sheets and has to get up to cool down. In those sleepless hours her mind returns to the married friends who don't call her and her own divorce years ago. It's no wonder that she's tired, and so at work, she struggles to deal with the demands of the new role she's taken on. When she gets home, her mum calls to arrange a family reunion and Lucy explodes with irritation: 'Mum, I just can't think about this now. Why is it always me you get to help you? My brother's the one you should ask. You never ask him for help, and he never offers. He's so lazy!'

Lucy puts down the phone, takes a drink of tea and breathes deeply. I just lost it on the phone, she thinks. And it wasn't the first time. She remembers her fury when someone cut in front of her car earlier that day and her curtness to her oh-so-chatty colleague. In fact, her anger is still boiling inside her now. She thinks that none of this is fair: her job problems, her lack of sleep, the way her mother expects so much of her, her brother's laziness and even her temper.

This isn't the person she wants to be, and it isn't the person she used to be. Her Bible remains closed on the table in front of her and she feels no desire to open it and read about what she knows she should be doing. Feeling wretched and guilty and frustrated, Lucy reaches for another chocolate biscuit.

Later that night, in the Bible study Lucy couldn't avoid, she realised that the struggle of her heart wasn't with family, or careless drivers, or uncaring friends, or the menopause but with her desire to be in control of things around her, to have things the way she wants. In her outburst she had given up trying to control her tongue because her world felt out of her control. She remembered the bitter truth of Jesus' words, 'Nothing outside a person can defile them by going into them. Rather, it is what comes out of a person that defiles them ... it is from within, out of a person's heart, that evil thoughts come' (Mk. 7:15, 21).

Of course, the truth that Lucy remembered didn't mean that it was wrong for her to feel unhappy that her brother expected her to do all the work in making family events run smoothly. It was unfair, had gone on too long, and needed dealing with. But the fury which rose up in her, and the shouted words of frustration weren't an attempt to put things right, rather they were a bellow of impatience that things weren't right just then. She wanted it all to be all right, and all her way.

The Triple-H-Threat bearing down on Lucy that day didn't make her lash out, though it exerted a heavy pressure on her heart. She was discovering what Martin Luther, four centuries before had described: 'tribulation does not make people impatient but proves that they are impatient, so everyone may learn from tribulation how his heart is constituted'.[7] Her heart itself, weary of putting up with things, and filling up with a desire for control, had brought about that sinful shout. She had seen in this small tribulation what her sinful heart was really like.

The heart-ease we need

Having seen the 'constitution' of her own heart, what should Lucy do? What about Sasha, overwhelmed by everything and conscious of how she'd been shouting at her daughter, again. What should you do when you are reminded again of your weakness and proneness to sin? There are plenty of sensible ideas which might help us cope better. Looking after our bodies can help our mental health, and this can put us in a better place to deal with our spiritual needs. God has made you a whole person, and he cares about your body, mind and soul.

This means it's worth considering the gifts he has given us to live well. Exercise has been shown to help mood disorders and can really help with the sleep problems that come in midlife. And there's data to prove that being out in a green space may also make a real difference. Herbal remedies and B vitamins can certainly relieve some menopause symptoms, and talking therapy or simple friendship can help us think through the pressures we're under and the way we manage them. HRT too, is a gift, which can balance our moods, as are other types of prescription medication.

All these are good things provided by our heavenly Father. They can calm us down and help us see clearly. But the best gift, and the only gift which truly heals the heart, is Jesus. He is the doctor who has come for those who are spiritually sick; he is the one we need to see.

The first-century Christians in Colossae were under threat. They were being tempted by false teachers to add religious rules onto the gospel of repentance and faith they had embraced. Their situation was vastly different from the one we're in today, but the advice Paul gave them on dealing with destabilising threats to faith is still relevant for us. He instructs them to 'set' their 'hearts on' – that is desire or seek – 'things above, where Christ is, seated at the right hand of God' and to 'Set' their 'minds on things above, not on earthly things' (Col. 3:1–2).

This is the advice Lucy and Sasha need, and that we need, too, when we are feeling overwhelmed by irritation and unruly anger, or anxiety and pessimistic thoughts. Such turmoil, no matter whether it is triggered by hormones, habitat or hurt, is often marked by a feeling that things are dangerously or unfairly out of control. When we look to heaven, we see the loving Lord enthroned and reigning.

It's a relief to look up, but to set ourselves determinedly, persistently – in both our feelings and in our thinking – on

Christ might seem too hard. If you're anything like me, concentration can be a struggle, and you may have plenty of memories of fresh starts and keen bursts in the Christian life which have petered out. It can be tempting to think, 'Why bother? I'll just dry up again.'

Paul gives us the answer to this question. We can look up because we are already there: 'you have been raised with Christ' (Col. 3:1). Through faith in Christ, believers are *so* united to him, that *they* have 'died with Christ' (Col. 2:20). All that *he* has gone through is *theirs*, which means that their sin – mine, yours, Sasha's, Lucy's – has already been punished when Jesus experienced God's rightful anger at human rebellion on the cross. Lucy's frustration that at 48 she should know better than to speak to mum like a teenager, can be replaced by a relief that she is forgiven. That even this grubby, embarrassing sin is paid for. Sasha's shame at her volatile reactions and self-pity can give way to praise that she is loved and welcomed in.

Seventeenth-century pastor Thomas Goodwin says that the believer's 'very sins move [Jesus] to pity more than to anger'.[8] How wonderful! The high and holy one, in all his purity, looks at his child with tenderness. When we are overwhelmed by turbulent emotions and blame ourselves or our circumstances or the menopause for our hidden feelings or public outbursts, we must pause and remember our Lord's great tenderness, and turn to him.

Paul wants the Colossians to know that being united to Christ in his death and resurrection, brings complete safety.

Christians' lives are so 'hidden with Christ in God' (Col. 3:3), that Paul can say he 'is your life' (Col. 3:4). Just as chicks are hidden under the mother hen's wing, so the believer's life is kept out of danger's way. Neither Satan's attacks nor God's own righteous judgement can dislodge the believer from his care. As we lift the eyes of our hearts to his ruling love, and know that we are held within that love, we find the still point in a whirling world.

Four hundred years ago, a monk spelt out the wonder of this acceptance:

> *The King, full of mercy and goodness, very far from chastising me, embraces me with love, makes me eat at His table, serves me with His own hands, gives me the key of His treasures; He …. delights Himself with me incessantly … and treats me in all respects as His favourite.*[9]

More important than any believer's status as an employee, or wife, or parent, or daughter in an earthly family is the reality that she is eternally united to Christ, adopted as a precious child of God. When midlife upends our emotions and makes us wonder along with Sasha who we are, or makes us impatient with being taken for granted, as Lucy experienced, drinking in this truth provides the real medicine we need.

The action we need to take

These definite descriptions of every Christian are not only sweet comfort, they also empower practical change. It's our status as 'God's chosen people, holy and dearly loved' (Col. 3:12), which means we have already 'taken off [our] old self … and have put on the new self' (Col. 3:9–10). I may feel as though I slip and slide around, but *in* Christ I *am* a new person, and now I'm called to live like it (Col. 3:5–17). And wonderfully, because Christians are *in* Christ, we must, and can live like him. Because we're united to him, his character will be taking root in us.

Living like Jesus begins with the discipline of setting our minds and hearts on things above, not only in the crises, but in our everyday routines. It is a fact that the majority of Western Christians come to faith in childhood or teenage years. This means that by the age of 45 they have heard thousands of sermons and been told innumerable times to pray and read their Bibles. If you have met Christ later on in life, the language of 'quiet time' or 'devotional' may be less familiar. But whether we're new or old in faith, this basic building block of the Christian life is what we need. Although it might seem too simple an answer, or too hard to achieve when life is under pressure, or an idea that only induces guilt, if we want to taste the comfort of our union with Christ, we must develop a habit of setting our hearts and minds on him.

Discipline might be the word we least want to hear when we're struggling emotionally, or if we feel as though we've failed. We want hot chocolate for the soul, not a boot camp. But the experience of generations of Christians is that good habits provide sweetness. Pastor Joe Barnard talks about HIIT (High Intensity Interval Training – exercising in highly focused short bursts) as a good way of thinking about our devotional lives.[10]

A short burst of proper concentration is better than a long time of distraction. Putting away your phone and taking up a pen and notebook to write down thoughts and prayers might help. Or praying out loud and even standing up or kneeling down can all help to focus our minds. You might want to listen to an audio Bible. Or if your mood is very low and you're exhausted, just take one short verse and repeat it as you drive to work or walk the dog or cook dinner, until you know it by heart and it becomes your prayer. It is worth doing whatever it takes to set our minds and hearts on the one who has saved us.

We all make time to brush our teeth every day, and by middle age we probably have a good habit of making our beds and washing up. Spending time feeding on God's Word and praying in response is no less important. And just as an exercise routine is hard to make and easy to break, so is a routine of spending time with God. You may be upended by life events – illness or sudden crisis, or even the disorder of going on holiday – and fall out of the habit. The right response is not self-blame but crying out to God for help to begin again.

You can pray, 'Lord, my heart is cold, give me a desire for your Word.' You can be honest: 'Jesus, I can't concentrate, help me to focus right now' or 'Lord I feel furious, I don't know what to do, please help me see you.' You can ask for energy when you're exhausted and self-control when you're distracted, and you can even plead for faith when you feel all your trust has ebbed away.

The good news is that Jesus promises to give the good gift of the Holy Spirit when we ask in faith; so when we ask for his help, those prayers will certainly be answered. In his strength, we will be able to set our moody hearts and our unsettled minds on things above where he is seated in the heavenly realms. And we will find him to be our help and refuge.

Reflection:

1. What are the Triple-H-Threats (your hormones, your habitat and the hurts you've experienced) which are troubling you at the moment? What are the battles within your heart to take God at his Word?

2. Take time to pray through each item you've written down, asking the Lord to help you understand what you're feeling and to give you wisdom to address each matter in a way that honours him.

3. How are you setting your mind on things above? Is there anything you can change which might help you focus more frequently and more joyfully on how securely you're united to Christ?

Chapter 4

* * *

Who Cares What I Look Like?

* * *

Coping with my changing face

Boots the Chemist, the UK's best-known seller of beauty products, stocks a total of 363 anti-ageing products. From the magical 'Youth Activating Concentrate' to the scarily scientific 'Hyaluronic Acid Serum', these products promise to somehow interrupt our ageing, if only we will spend and spend and spend.

Of course, we all know that stopping isn't really possible: we are getting older, and it shows. But perhaps we still end up paying more for the moisturiser with the added retinol or another promising elixir because we'll take a chance on anything that might at least slow the drooping and drying of our skin. Mariella Frostrup writes, 'I sometimes still experience tangible shockwaves at the sight of my wrinkled face' and recalls seeing herself at 50 as 'wizened

... a shocker'.[1] The truth is seeing signs of ageing in our bodies can bring a kind of grief and panic, and this is what cosmetic companies profit from.

Perhaps you've had similar feelings? I know I have. Whether it's wrinkles, or liver spots, or our hair – now strangely sprouting on our faces and turning grey and unruly on our heads – we can sometimes catch sight of ourselves and see 'a shocker', too. And then guilt can quickly follow. After all, doesn't it sound vain to be preoccupied by appearances or even self-hating to be judging oneself like this? We're in an enlightened era that's definitely anti-ageism, so surely we should accept the changes of getting older?

The secular answer is a paradox. Yes, you should 'accept yourself' but you should also work hard to 'adapt yourself'. Mariella commends a list of 1. Botox; 2. expensive cream; 3. a great hairdresser handy with dye; and 4. fashionable but not too revealing clothes. She pays lip service to the mantra of self-acceptance – celebrate the real you! – yet all the while labouring to cover up the real signs of age. It's back to spend, spend, spend!

This isn't much help for Helen. She's hit her early 50s and is feeling drab. Her late 20s and her 30s were devoted to caring for her three children and then, in her mid-40s, she was in an accident which permanently affected her mobility and meant she had to reduce the hours she works in the local supermarket. When Helen gets to church on a Sunday, she feels she doesn't fit in. It's full of young families and students and their lives seem so vibrant compared to hers. She's not got much to say, even if they did bother to come and chat with her. Her husband tells her not to worry, things will get better, but she's not convinced they will.

Helen's clothes are old, she knows, but money is tight and, to tell the truth, she's never been that bothered by fashion. The problem is much bigger than that; she feels altogether worn out and unattractive. There's no wonder people give me a wide berth, she thinks. And what could change? It isn't just her wardrobe that looks tired, her face does, and her mind feels it too. She has time on her hands, because of her health restrictions, and what people at church and even her husband don't really know is how much of this time is spent online. She's bored and weary, and so 'next episode' is clicked very often on her laptop.

There's so much out there that draws her in, whether searching for bargains or daydreaming about craft projects she'd undertake if she had more energy, or just watching re-runs of her favourite comedy series. In theory she's resting and none of what she's consuming is bad, but somehow it doesn't refresh her. It sucks her in, and sucks life out of her, at the same time.

Helen has always been taught that what matters is what's on the inside, and she tries to remember that, when she's struggling with these feelings. It's just that what's on the inside doesn't seem all that special to her. Neither Botox nor an expensive haircut are within Helen's reach, and it's not what she wants, either. Accepting and adapting just aren't enough to deal with the way that she feels about her appearance and what she feels these physical changes have done to her identity.

Fading out

Helen feels largely invisible, and she isn't alone in experiencing this as a negative consequence of middle age. A recent study showed that by the time they are 52 years old, 70 per cent of women fear their ageing makes them feel, 'unseen, over-looked, and patronized'.[2] This isn't a new phenomenon; Clarissa in the 1920s novel *Mrs Dalloway*, 'had the oddest sense of being herself invisible, unseen; unknown' as she went shop-ping.[3] What these women – fictional and real – are expressing is a fear that as their faces lose their youthful glow, an indicator of fertility and sexual attractiveness, they appear irrelevant not only to those who are younger, but sometimes even to their own age group. One cynical journalist claims, 'wrinkles have a way of making women disappear, one crease at a time'.[4]

For Clarissa Dalloway, invisibility allowed a kind of freedom, and perhaps that is something you'd welcome too. She could walk round London observing others, but not being observed herself.

But today we are told that to have a strong sense of self we need to be acknowledged and celebrated by others, and that to be sidelined is unjust discrimination. More than this, it seems common to all people, everywhere, however shy, that we need to be valued, and to be valued, we need to be seen. Helen feels unnoticed at church and by her grown children; whatever Bible truths she knows in her head, and whatever her husband says, seeming invisible makes her feel undervalued, even unloved.

But there's another reason why noticing the wrinkles arrive on our faces can make us grieve. The desire for beauty is common to all humans. We don't just want to be seen, but also to see. We yearn for beauty. We travel far afield to view mountains or famous paintings, and when we get there, we marvel. At weddings we love watching the bride and groom transfixed by each other, splendid in beautiful clothes. We coo over sleeping babies, with their flawless skin and tiny, perfect hands.

One theologian says that through this 'unexpected charge of delight ... We may ... be reminded of the goodness of God's creation and the extravagance of God's care.'[5] To enjoy beauty is a very good thing. But when youth is associated with beauty, and symmetry and smoothness are desired, sagging skin and frown lines can look ugly to us, bringing distaste rather than delight.

Both these reasons, perhaps, are why plenty of A-listers have gone under the knife multiple times in an attempt to reclaim the evenness of the features and tautness of their faces. They want to keep being visible through being beautiful. The problem with this radical action, as seen in plenty of snide media comments, is that it often doesn't work; it results in what philosopher Kathleen Stott calls, 'moulding a death-mask out of still-living flesh', creating a frozen picture where we expect life and movement.[6] The truth is, we can't stop time, and our attempts to manufacture beauty and significance in ourselves, in defiance of time, so often result in something pitiful.

Some of us might look down on those stars and the other ordinary people who invest hard-earned money in trying to stop time's gravitational pull through the surgeon's knife. It's certainly easy to scoff when their faces end up looking fake. But perhaps we should be more sympathetic. The God-given delight in beauty is common to all of us, as we've seen, and no wonder, because it's a hallmark of our Maker, the God who is beautiful, and who makes beautiful things.

Along with climbing mountains or visiting art galleries or admiring babies, we want to look well too. Some of us dye our hair; some wear make-up. We may select our clothes carefully, not wanting to seem, in that horrid phrase, 'mutton-dressed-as-lamb' nor wanting to look like our grandmothers, either. Like other God-given desires, though, this hunger for beauty is broken. Often, rather than bringing us delight, it results in anxiety or self-concern and instead of pointing us to our beautiful Lord, it even takes some into destructive idolatry.

So, we live in tension. Many of us are happy to stay out of the lime-light and none of us wants to be on the receiving end of unwanted attention. We perhaps worry that being concerned with outward beauty is vain, and yet we want to be beautiful, and we don't want to be overlooked. Helen, despite not caring too much about fashion and wanting to live a quiet life, still longs to be seen and to look alive. And that's okay. It is good to want to look good. The truth is that we shouldn't be content with fading away and becoming invisible because he has made us to be seen and to see. The Lord has designed us, ultimately, for beauty's older and greater relative: glory.

Seeing and being seen

The word beauty doesn't appear that often in the Bible, but glory does. Its Hebrew form, *Kavod*, implies not only brightness, but also weight or significance. Glory is the outward display of God's own self. It is blindingly beautiful, but there's more to it than something lovely-looking or impressive. Think back to the time when Moses asks God to 'show me your glory' (Ex. 33:18). The Lord graciously responds: 'I will cause all my goodness to pass in front of you, and I will proclaim my name, the LORD, in your presence' (Ex. 33:19).

The power of God's holy presence is so great that Moses is hidden in a rock for protection. Then the Lord comes down and proclaims:

> *The LORD, the LORD, the compassionate and gracious*
> *God, slow to anger, abounding in love and faithfulness,*
> *maintaining love to thousands, and forgiving wickedness,*
> *rebellion and sin. (Ex. 34:6–7)*

This is an extraordinary moment. But it's only one of many of God's self-displays in the Old Testament. And in most of them, he turns up uninvited. In Genesis 16, Hagar has fled into the desert, pregnant by her master and mistreated by her mistress. There God appears, and he treats her with compassion. This woman who has not been taken seriously or properly considered at all, names him El Roi, 'the God who sees me' (Gen. 16:13). Hagar, like Moses, sees God because he has first seen her.

Hagar's story changes through this encounter. She obeys his voice and leaves the vulnerability of the desert. Here lies great comfort for the many women who have been mistreated and sidelined, and those who feel worn out and unimportant, as Helen and so many others do too.

C.S. Lewis puts it like this: 'perhaps it seems rather crude to describe glory as the fact of being "noticed" by God. But … St. Paul promises to those who love God not, as we should expect, that they will know Him, but that they will be known by Him.'[7] When he sees us, it is not a superficial glance or a dismissive scan, but a deep and full understanding of who we are and where we are.

We survive this scrutiny because we are hidden in a rock, just as Moses was. As we saw in the last chapter, Christians are united to Christ, 'hidden' in him (Col. 3:3), safe and secure. The fact that God sees us in this way means we have significance, no matter how faded our outer appearance or how much our hearts are spoilt by sin. He doesn't turn away or dismiss us when we reach midlife and menopause, even if others do; he looks at us in love.

The God who embraces ugliness

We can feel sure of this kind welcome from God because 2,000 years ago the Lord Jesus didn't just look at humanity from afar but became like us, in all our mundane ordinariness. Isaiah foresaw this when he said, 'He had no beauty or majesty to attract us to him, nothing in his appearance that we should desire him' (Is. 53:2). And he did this to show us the extent of his love in action.

The Lord Jesus embraced everyday, even unattractive, flesh which aged and grew tired and achy. Violence and humiliation made him literally unsightly: 'He was despised and rejected by mankind ... Like one from whom people hide their faces' (Is. 53:3). More than that, Jesus himself describes these last few hours of his mortal life as the very time 'the Son of Man is glorified, and God is glorified in him' (Jn. 13:31).

It's an extraordinary paradox, that at his ugliest, Jesus was truly displaying his glorious beauty. Not the glory of his resurrection body or the illumined brightness Peter, James and John saw so briefly at the transfiguration, but the visible demonstration of his staggering love for his people and his righteous, loving obedience to his Father. At the cross, he was ugly, made 'to be sin for us' (2 Cor. 5:21). In Christ's tortured face, you see glory more clearly than even Moses did. We see God's deep, deep love and his hatred for sin, united in sacrifice. He has seen us in our sin, and marvellously, by becoming sin, he makes us fit to see him in his glory.

The horror show of the cross tells us something about how to rightly view our ageing faces in a world that values superficial beauty. Jesus took on the ordinariness of decaying human flesh and the ugliness of our sin, so that we could not only be seen and known by him, but, in C.S. Lewis' words, we could please him:

> To please God ... to be a real ingredient in the divine happiness ... to be loved by God, not merely pitied, but delighted in as an artist delights in his work or a father in a son – [this] seems impossible, a weight or burden of glory which our thoughts can hardly sustain. But so it is.[8]

Being delighted in like this transforms us. It not only is glorious but endows us with glory; we are given a radiance way beyond our human understandings of beauty.

Beautified by unfading glory

May 2023 saw the coronation of a man, Charles Windsor. In the ceremony, his grand clothes were taken from him. He was stripped down to a plain and simple shirt. He looked in that moment like any old man in a nightgown. But then he was dressed, covered with glorious robes and a crown: he was shown to be His Majesty Charles III, a royal ruler.

These rituals weren't just dreamed up, they were taken from symbols in the Bible, and they speak, not about political leadership in the UK, but about the shape of Christ's life. He first laid aside his splendour, as he took on human form, but then wonderfully he was exalted and glorified. And as believers are united to him, this is their destiny too. Though her everyday life may look unspectacular, Helen is connected to Christ, so is headed towards a coronation and a wonderful transformation. And so are you.

In Romans, Paul makes the connection between Christ's glorification and ours:

> *For those God foreknew he also predestined to be*
> *conformed to the image of his Son ... And those*
> *he predestined, he also called; those he called, he*
> *also justified; those he justified, he also glorified.*
> *(Rom. 8:29–30)*

The second sentence is a fleshing out of the first; to be glorified is, through the justifying work of Jesus on the cross, to be conformed to the image of Christ.

Paul presents this to us in the past tense. If we are united to Christ, then in one very real sense we have already been glorified through that union. And that brings a future certainty: Christians will receive a glorified body after Christ has returned, a body which is recognisably their own, yet radically different from this earthly one, because of its immortality and power. It will be what a friend of mine calls an upgrade.[9] Whether we are lamenting the lines on our faces, or resigned to feeling frumpy, then this is good news. It is good news, however, not because we will then finally feel satisfied with our looks but because the glory we will be clothed in will reflect all glory back to Christ. The entrapping vanity and self-concern about our appearance will be gone. We will simply be sharers in his self-giving beauty. Hallelujah!

And this glorification process is going on right now, too. In Colossians 3 we learn that our new self 'is being renewed in knowledge in the image of its Creator' (Col. 3:10). Rather than the new self being spoilt through time as we mess up, it is being refreshed as the Holy Spirit teaches us about Christ. Rather than shrinking over time, as our bodies do, 'the believer's new nature resembles a growing plant'.[10] And this extraordinary growth comes through the work of the Holy Spirit showing us more of Christ; as we understand more of him, so our desires and behaviours change. As we see him, so we can become like him.

Battling for beauty

There's a simple solution then, to our complex feelings about our looks and how people look at us. It is to focus our attention on Christ. Paul says, 'we all, who with unveiled faces contemplate the Lord's glory, are being transformed into his image with ever-increasing glory, which comes from the Lord, who is the Spirit' (2 Cor. 3:18).[11] Contemplation of Christ, through soaking in and chewing over God's Word by the Spirit's power, makes for growing glorification.

To be made more like Jesus – to show more self-control, gentleness, faithfulness, goodness, kindness, patience, peace, joy and love – is to reflect in an 'ever-increasing' manner, his bright and holy beauty. We might be tempted to think that this contemplation must *feel* kind of floaty and radiant, and perhaps even effortless. But Helen finds it hard. And it is. To think it should be easy is to forget how Christ lived. Again and again in the New Testament, writers associate focusing on Christ and becoming more like him with struggle.

Helen has plenty of hardship in her life and it shows: her limited mobility brings daily restrictions and will continue to for the rest of her life. But such suffering doesn't replace the call to 'put to death ... whatever belongs to your earthly nature' even as we set our minds and hearts on things above (Col. 3:1–4). Paul lists 'sexual immorality, impurity, lust, evil desires and greed, which is idolatry' (Col. 3:5) as targets for execution. Longings for and pursuit of anything ahead of God is to be killed. For some this might be porn or fantasies, shopping or comfort eating. For Helen, it's the habitual internet grazing and TV watching.

And, of course, it is also that preoccupation with self-image. Some of us are endlessly aiming to look good in front of others and ourselves, to protect ourselves from shame. For others, including Helen, it's a negative preoccupation; as she looks within, feels frustrated with her outward image and doubts her worth.

All these God-substitutes are fading pleasures, idols which make us smaller and weaker. Contemplating Christ instead, strengthens us to say no to them and to live for him. Remembering he sees us and loves us, makes us bigger. It enables us to stop and turn off the screen, or to walk out of the kitchen. Thinking of him distracts our thoughts from ourselves and turns them outwards to him and to others.

So, beautiful Christlikeness comes through enduring hardship and battling against sin. This is how Jesus travelled the earthly path to his exaltation, so it is no wonder that this should be our journey too. He was rejected, afflicted and tempted, and at times, we are too. We fix our eyes on him to learn how to persevere in the struggles of the Christian life; and fixing our eyes on him will lead to yet more struggles as see more clearly what our lives should look like. But we're not on our own. God's desire for and delight in our transformation means that he is with us in the battle. Day by day, we face the realities of sin and temptation, and hear the call to put sin to death (Col. 3:5), and day by day he gives us power, by his Holy Spirit to fight.

As Helen remembers Jesus' care for his church, she acts. Rather than using her laptop for watching re-runs, she can send a message to her older friend from church and reach out to a young mum from the congregation and offer help. And she can pray, for her neighbours, for the world. Her clothes and hairstyle haven't changed, she still looks 52, but she is being changed. The dullness which she feared made her uninteresting, has been replaced by the interest she shows in others, and it shines.

Our grey crown of glory

At a conference a little while ago, a younger friend told me how excited she was to be getting a few grey hairs. I don't think it was because she thought silver locks were cool, but because she'd remembered a verse from Proverbs which says grey hair is 'a crown of glory' (Prov. 16:31, ESV). Because she was a godly woman, she wanted that glory! Having more than a few grey hairs myself, I had less enthusiasm than her, and her words made me go back to what Solomon was saying. Was I being worldly in not embracing my own emerging 'crown'?

As I compared these verses, and thought elsewhere about crowns, I saw that we were both right. Grey hair here is just a symbol – it's not wrong to dye it out – but what it signifies is important; ageing is a good thing for Christian women. It is a sign of spiritual battles won and progress in godliness. That is a liberating thought. Rather than grieving over evidence that we are decaying, we can really celebrate each reminder that even as we age outwardly, by the help of the Holy Spirit, we are becoming more like Jesus, and in fact, we can't have the one without the other.

Growing to be like Jesus takes time. And it takes effort. And it usually involves pain. But as we take this discipline of gazing on him and warring against sin, so his reflected glory shines more and more. The struggle will show on our faces, but Jesus will show in our souls.

Reflection:

1. In what ways is your self-worth tied to the way you see yourself, and the way you think others see you? Are there aspects of your attitude which you need to repent of or require help to change?

2. How does knowing that you are seen by God, and that his powerful Holy Spirit is in you, change the way you act and think in the slack moments of the day, or when you are anxious or lonely?

3. Take time to reflect slowly on these verses, considering the beauty of Christ and his gospel:

He grew up before him like a tender shoot,
and like a root out of dry ground.
He had no beauty or majesty to attract us to him,
nothing in his appearance that we should desire him.
He was despised and rejected by mankind,
a man of suffering, and familiar with pain.
Like one from whom people hide their faces
he was despised, and we held him in low esteem.
Surely he took up our pain
and bore our suffering,
yet we considered him punished by God,
stricken by him, and afflicted.
But he was pierced for our transgressions,
he was crushed for our iniquities;
the punishment that brought us peace was on him,
and by his wounds we are healed. (Is. 53:2–5)

Chapter 5

* * *

How Can I Care for Them All?

* * *

Managing the family sandwich

Google 'middle-aged woman + family' and you get some surprising results. There are news stories of women who have recently given birth; a link to an article on dating at a 'mature age', and a story about grandparenthood. There's nothing about the complex family relationships that most of us seem to have acquired by the time we meet middle age.

It's highly likely you will have at least one parent who is in his or her 70s by the time you're in your mid-40s, and you may well have school-aged children too. Move on five years to the point at which menopause will probably be in full swing, and you could well have teenagers or young adults still at home, plus one or two parents or parents-in-law getting into their 80s. Another five years, and many of us will be combining some amount of care for aged relatives with grandchildren.[1]

Of course, things may be good: right now your parents could be a great support to you, taking some of the strain. Your kids might be fun to hang out with and help with chores. But you could be divorced, dealing with a teenager with serious mental health problems and a parent who has just been diagnosed with dementia. You may be a single parent, or an only child, or part of a large and argumentative family. Your parents might be hostile to your faith, or they may live on a different continent. Your kids could be pre-teens struggling at school, or in their 20s and needing financial help. They might just be regular kids who need a lot of time and love.

The shape and context of our families vary widely, but almost all will include some tension that peaks as we reach middle age. The language of 'sandwich generation' makes sense; we're stuck in the middle, and as in some sandwiches I've eaten, the filling can feel small and squashed. Abigail, a single parent with children at home, full time work and very frail parents, says she often feels like 'it's all been sucked out of me'.

Of course, women bearing the burden of caring for older and younger family members is nothing new. Elizabeth Prentiss in the early nineteenth century memorably described the spiritual pressures of this in her book *Stepping Heavenward*, and it has been the theme of plenty of secular novels ever since, from Dickens to Anne Tyler. Husbands, brothers and sons are involved in many cases (estimated to shoulder the burden of 30 per cent of non-professional care for older relatives), but more often than not, it is women who both voluntarily, and because of family or wider cultural expectations, end up doing more of the juggling.[2]

Unmarried women often find that their parents anticipate far more of them than their brothers or married sisters, though they may well be dealing with the same life pressures without the help of a spouse. The bright pictures of middle-aged women in the media, girl-bossing it in the boardroom or looking immaculate in their gorgeous homes, just don't match up with the reality of life for the many who are in the middle of the sandwich.

Feeling torn

Abigail doesn't feel empowered or immaculate as she fills in forms and has yet another call with social services trying to find a way to increase care visits for her dad. He's now 85 and had a stroke five months ago which has left him with cognitive damage. Abigail's 80-year-old mum isn't coping very well with the care her husband now needs; she's just not physically strong enough any longer to do much of the work.

So, every other weekend Abigail drives down to help. She does laundry as she now often finds them in dirty clothes, and puts meals in the freezer as she suspects they're not eating very well. She calms her dad, who gets frequently agitated, does the shopping, and tries to talk her mum into accepting more help. By Sunday afternoon when she gets back, she's exhausted. Her friends tell her she's mad, that she should insist her parents move into a home, yet Abigail feels torn. These are her parents, they gave so much for her, she should surely give to them now.

But every time she drives down to Hampshire, she feels guilty for leaving her twins behind with friends, especially as they're facing exams, and then every time she gets a phone call from her panicking mum, she feels guilty for not helping more. She's just about managing to keep up with her work as an administrator; at home, though, order has gone awry, she's forgetting messages from the children's school, and her previously tidy home is a mess.

As for church, she barely knows what's going on any longer and has had to drop off the children's team, which she loved. On top of all this, she has started to have night sweats, waking up pretty damp at least a couple of times each night, and then struggling to get back to sleep because of all the stress swirling round her brain. Most of her waking hours panic feels barely a breath away and she wonders how much longer she can go on.

Underlying all this for Abigail and the many like her, including those who are married or don't have their own kids, is the grief that her parents are now dependent on her; a reversal has taken place, and she now really is the adult in the room. Comedian Jenny Éclair comments that we go from secretly thinking that our parents will 'kiss it all better', to realising that 'the problems you're faced with [are the] big ones – the life-and-death ones, the ones you don't have any answers for, and certainly not the ones that can be kissed better.'[3] It's good news, then, that the Bible actually gives us many answers in the pain of life, as well as comfort and principles which can help us address the competing demands for attention and care and the agonising choices we sometimes face.

For the Lord

Before we look at some of the nitty gritty of how to survive, and what practical actions we need to take when we are feeling squeezed, it's worth asking a more basic question: Why should we love our nearest and dearest? Paul's words in Colossians 3 speak about the networks of relationships we all exist within. He gives us some clear answers which go beyond the 'they're so gorgeous', or 'it's your duty' – a relief when they're being far from lovely and quite which duty comes first is hard to decide.

Having given the church instructions about how to speak and worship, Paul provides a simple cover-all approach to life: 'And whatever you do, whether in word or deed, do it all in the name of the Lord Jesus, giving thanks to God the Father through him' (Col. 3:17). It won't fit neatly on a wristband like 'What Would Jesus Do', but it is a sensible life-motto, if we can understand and apply it.

To act and speak in the name of Christ obviously doesn't mean acting how we want and branding it Jesus-approved. We must show the world what Jesus is really like in our lives. Wonderfully, however, this call to do everything 'in the name of the Lord Jesus', also means acting in the power that he so generously gives.[4] It should stop us in our tracks to ask, 'Can I represent God in this? Is this action or speech reflecting what he is like?' And it pushes us forward; if the answer to those questions is 'yes', we can say, 'He is with me in this hard task that honours him.'

Paul then applies this general rule to precisely those relationships which can prove painful in midlife. Ann Benton writes about this in her fantastic book about caring for an older relative: 'older doesn't always mean wiser. And it hardly ever means more winsome.'[5] She is honest about the grumpiness and thanklessness she encountered as she spent hours each day caring for her parents-in-law, as well as the physical exhaustion and unpleasantness it entailed. Bed baths and cleaning soiled clothes, 'did not feel noble, it felt demeaning'.[6]

Anyone involved in care, whether for children or adults, will recognise this reality. As a parent of two special needs children, Andrew Wilson, says 'Some days we just look at our lives and think *this is awful*. And sometimes it is.'[7] Ann needed the motivation of Colossians 3:20, where Paul tells children to obey their parents because it 'pleases the Lord'. As we grow into adulthood, we are still called to honour our parents, and this still honours Christ. Ann's efforts did not bring her pleasure that often, nor did it always satisfy them. But it was representing Jesus, and she was empowered by him. He saw and was pleased.

Likewise, if you are a parent, Paul gives you clear instructions both here, and in the parallel passage in Ephesians 6. He speaks to fathers but this incorporates all parents; they must not 'embitter' or 'exasperate' their children, or they will be 'discouraged' (Col. 3:21). This can be extremely hard when teenagers are stormy and rude, when they take us for granted or make decisions which lead them into danger. But rather than lash out at them, or moan about them to others, rather than letting tension and resentment build, we remember God has given us a vital role in their lives. Parents must bring up their children in the 'training and instruction of the Lord' (Eph. 6:4).

In the same way we treat our parents with respectful care because of Christ, so we show great care in how we treat children. God has put children in almost all our lives – whether our own children, those in our extended family or church, or our godchildren – that Christ might be represented and so honoured. If you are looking after children with mental or physical health issues, which drain your energy to the bottom, then this instruction is especially refreshing. You cannot possibly do everything that might be good for your child, but you can do this: encourage and teach them about Christ.

Alongside the call to parent well and honour parents, Paul also calls for obedience to employers and right marriage relationships. These can be hard.

Not only is there so much to juggle in midlife that a marriage can be neglected, but shifting identity and changing bodies can bring pressure to the relationship. Menopause can very often diminish libido as well as affect physical aspects of sex, while changing moods and self-perception can make it easy to question previously established attitudes and habits.[8]

In the light of this, Paul's command to wives to 'submit' to their husbands (Col. 3:18) can be hard to embrace. And yet it is a command which, rightly understood, allows for the flourishing of marriage even in the often-difficult years of midlife. That's because this submission is to be 'as is fitting in the Lord' (Col. 3:18) and is mirrored by the husbands' responsibility to 'love your wives and do not be harsh with them' (Col. 3:19).

Just as we serve our parents and our children to please God, so in our marriages, we are to act in a way that pleases God. This means generously and wisely, but not slavishly or fearfully. A Christian wife can't be everything to her husband – God needs to be his 'all in all', not us – but she can point her husband to Jesus as she reflects her Saviour's gentleness and care. Marriages change as time goes on, they evolve and adapt, but these commands of mutual love and submission, modelled by how Christ loves and serves, provide a secure framework in which we can work out that change.

Drawing lines

Aiming to please Christ can help us begin to discern a way through when we're torn between the inevitable conflicts that arise when multiple responsibilities weigh upon us.

Jesus is the one who can deal with all who come to him. He's the one who has made the final sacrifice, which means that his followers do not have to serve everyone's needs, nor commit themselves to silent martyrdom. We are not to do his job, but we are to seek his glory.

One friend of mine was dealing with her mother's terminal illness while her teenage son was experiencing a mental health crisis. As she sat with her sister by her mother's bedside, she felt torn. This looked like the right thing to do; her father was grateful and these were her mum's last, precious days. But though her son wouldn't talk to her and didn't want her around, she knew that he was in real need. She talked to her dad, prayed hard, and decided to halve her hospital visits so that she could be at home more of the time. Her conclusion was that it was more pleasing to God to be present for her son, despite his rejection, than to spend hours with her well-supported parents. Exposing herself in this way to a situation she couldn't control was difficult, but it threw her upon the Lord in a way she had never known before, and in the pain, she found his help.

Knowing that our motivation is for Christ to be honoured keeps us going when service is very hard, and it also helps us evaluate how much we should serve. It shifts us from any pride in our service and from feeling that we have to do it all. It's okay to confess that we just don't know the right thing to do or how to manage our priorities. There is no rigid tier system in the Christian economy of service, which dictates that always a spouse comes before children, who come before extended family, who come before church family, who come before colleagues, who come before neighbours. We live in complex networks of need and service, and so require spiritual wisdom to discern how to obey God's commands in the time and circumstances he has placed us in; in all these relationships, the priority is to honour God, not to simply please people.

J.C. Ryle's instruction is of comfort when we are at the end of our energy or understanding: 'do not glory in your own faith, your own feelings, your own knowledge or your own diligence. Glory in nothing but Christ.'[9] When Abigail was on the motorway yet again, this very truth came to her. She realised that she'd been putting her confidence in her own knowledge and hard work. She'd felt as if she should be her parents' saviour. But, of course, she could never be that! As she prayed in the car for her family, she felt some of the stress lift; she couldn't do it all, and she didn't need to do it all. Christ was enough for her, and for her parents, too.

Abigail knew that her resources were being stretched too thin, and this fresh remembrance of God's grace made all the difference. That morning she'd read how she had to 'clothe [herself] with compassion, kindness, humility, gentleness and patience' (Col. 3:12), and had felt nothing but a burden. But she had forgotten what came first. Prior to the list of commands for spouses, parents, children, and slaves and their masters, Paul had called all Christians

'God's chosen people, holy and dearly loved'. God's grace has bought us and holds us, and the resources for service come from him.

We don't have to 'dig deep' to find in ourselves resources for caring for the often unlovely. Instead we find them outside of ourselves. Jesus modelled these garments for us, in how he touched the lepers, drew close to those who were grieving and was patient with his followers in their greed and ignorance. We need to reach out and put on Christ's beautiful clothing of 'compassion, kindness, humility, gentleness and patience' (Col. 3:12). When yet again we are taken for granted or treated rudely, whether by children or adults, we can forbear and forgive and love (Col. 3:13–14), as we ask for the Holy Spirit's endless strength.

Having Christ as our motivation and our support will keep us tender, where a stoical sense of duty might make us cold and resentful. It will also help us to be resilient where a heart driven exclusively by sentimental feelings would give up. When Paul instructs slaves to do their work 'with all your heart, as working for the Lord' he gives them a further motive, 'since you know you will receive an inheritance from the Lord as a reward' (Col. 3:23–24). Rightly fulfilling our family responsibilities – unglamourous and, frankly, often unnoticed and unrewarding as they are – will be honoured by God in glory, as we obey and rely on him now.

The support staff you need
That realisation in the car marked a change in Abigail's

approach, and it wasn't just that she found herself relying more on Christ. She began to reach out to others for their help too. First, she remembered her parents' old church friends and rang round, asking if any of them could pop over to check on them once a week, just for half an hour, and a couple of them said yes. Then she found a food delivery service which could deliver wholesome meals. It wasn't much, but enough to mean that she felt okay to visit every three weeks instead of every fortnight, while she concentrated on sorting out a better professional care package.

Abigail knows how her parents now really look forward to those friends from church popping over regularly. She thinks about how kind Margaret is; how she loves to bring over fresh baking, and how her parents love to receive it, too. It helps to remind herself of this when she's tempted to feel guilty about not being there. Keeping on remembering that she doesn't have to have all the answers straightaway when her panicking mum calls brings some relief too.

The reality is, humans do best in community and in routines, with regular treats and breaks to look forward to; this is true when we are carers and when we are being cared for. So it is important for everyone – and certainly not ungodly – to establish the boundaries of our giving. It's worth planning carefully: what regular service can I sustain, how can I work with others, and what are the small and sweet things I can schedule which will bring joy to those family members who are weak?

Then, you can consider yourself: what are the routine things which will give you strength to keep on going? Whether a coffee with a friend once a week or getting a burst of exercise every other day, or watching a certain TV show at a set time; it's good to regularly put down your cares and recognise your needs.

Abigail was absolutely right to rope in others. The verses we've looked at from Colossians are not addressed to individual Christians, but to the whole Colossian church. It's together that we are loved and clothed with love and compassion. And these gifted garments are for use in the church. That means that if you are struggling, stuck in between the demands of family and work, the Lord has equipped your brothers and sisters with ways and means to help too.

Ann Benton testifies to this. She and her husband found that private carers were not reliable enough to care for her parents-in-law and so she took up the majority of the work, but church members came alongside her in support. She writes, 'the church supplied me with "Charlie's Angels", a group of Christian women who volunteered their support for me ... these ordinary Christians were a shining testimony to Jesus Christ, for whose sake they gladly gave their time and their love'.[10]

It doesn't just happen with older people. In another church, a young mum asked a depressed teenager to come and help out with her children and an older couple encouraged him to walk their dog. They had seen the pressure the teenager's parents were under and so were finding ways of coming alongside him to help.

So, if your life is settled at the moment, then look around. Who is there in the middle of a care sandwich in need of help? And look widely. It's often those who aren't shouting loudly who are the most in need. A one-off gift of a casserole may be great, but often those under significant pressure need reliable, regular help. That might involve taking their elderly mother out for coffee once a month or making a brief phone call every week at the same time. It could be doing a basket of ironing once a fortnight or providing an afternoon of respite care every couple of months. Small but meaningful kindnesses make a big difference.

However and whoever we are caring for in our family or the church's generational sandwich, we 'do it all in the name of the Lord Jesus, giving thanks to God the Father through him' (Col. 3:17). Gratitude is the hallmark of Christian care, and can transform the bleakest situation. Many secular people are great carers, kind-hearted and gentle in manner, but they have no one to give thanks to, and so no higher horizon on which to rest their eyes. Christians, however, in the midst of great pressure, can turn outwards. We are motivated by Christ, and empowered by his Holy Spirit, and as we receive this strength, our hearts can sing.

Reflection:

1. 'Whatever you do, work at it with all your heart, as working for the Lord, not for human masters, since you know that you will receive an inheritance from the Lord as a reward. It is the Lord Christ you are serving' (Col. 3:23–24). Are your duties just items on a list or burdens that make you feel guilty, or can you see them as a way of serving Christ? To what extent are you connecting your hard work of caring with your identity in Christ? Pause to give thanks to God for his grace which equips us to serve.

2. Take time to do a care audit. How are you honouring Christ by caring for those the Lord has given you a special responsibility for whether it is nieces and nephews, children, parents or spouse? Are there relationships that you are sidestepping? Or are you taking on too much and trying, unsuccessfully, to do it all?

3. What practical ways can you serve better (not necessarily more!)? Are there routines of help you can offer those in your church family or your natural family? Identify one or two new things or different ways of serving which might refresh others.

Chapter 6

* * *

What Should I Do Now?

* * *

Making the most of midlife

Katie spent her 20s and 30s juggling part-time work and raising her four children. Life seemed full on; she and her husband were heavily involved in a busy church and with their extended family who lived nearby. But in her mid-40s, crippling migraines caused by hormonal changes took over her life. She could no longer do paid work, and even managing the house was difficult. When pain permitted, she sank herself into God's Word, seeking some relief.

As Katie focused on familiar passages of scripture, new insights opened up. Though she'd been immersed in church life for years, running a kids' club, cooking meals and giving the elderly lifts, she was shaken by how radical God's promises are, and how intricate his plans. Katie's hunger for the Bible grew from a desire to find comfort and distraction from pain into a new amazement that God should speak to her, should reveal himself to her in the pages of his book.

She found that morning by morning she woke up wanting to see and hear more of him and his powerful words, to go beyond the familiar and explore texts she'd previously thought were dry or irrelevant. And as Katie read more, she started to pray more deeply, with more ambition and confidence than she had done in years.

Back to the beginning

Perhaps Katie's story leaves you feeling guilty, or even cold at heart. You're busy, just as Katie was, and your enthusiasm for God's Word more often than not ebbs rather than flows. You're there at church, but you find it hard to fit in a daily Bible time – in fact, you've not had a regular time in the Word for years, despite multiple new resolutions. As for praying, when there's a crisis you'll definitely pray, and you do pray most nights with your kids, but you could hardly say that you regularly pray in private.

It's very easy to grow 'weary in doing good' (Gal. 6:9). When this happens we can give up looking for opportunities to serve and our attempts at a devotional life become at best half-hearted. Cynicism sets in and leaves us not quite comfortable with our efforts but still resigned to just plodding on with little expectation. No wonder many in middle age daydream of a kitchen extension or the next holiday, about children leaving home or even what is 'better by far', eternity with Christ, but have checked out of the heart-demands and hopes of the Christian life right now.

There is help for you if you feel stuck like this. Going through the motions, or simply getting by spiritually, doesn't have to be your story from now on. In his poem, 'A Wreath', the seventeenth-century vicar George Herbert starts by offering God 'a wreath of praise', but quickly he acknowledges that just like the branches and flowers twisted into a wreath, his life is 'crooked and winding'. Despite the certainty of his divine destination, he realises his own ways on earth just seem to twist and turn.

So, he prays:

> *Give me simplicity, that I may live,*
> *So live … that I may know Thy ways,*
> *Know them and practise them: then shall I give*
> *For this poor wreath, give Thee a crown of praise.*[1]

His longing is for a simple and single-minded childlike faith he can enjoy, despite the messiness of experience and deceitfulness of the world. He wants to offer his Lord something better than tangled motives and compromised, half-hearted action. Maybe you desire this too? I know I do. Why not pray for it, as George Herbert did, perhaps with trusted friends, seeking God together for his Spirit's refreshing and refining power. This is one of the best kinds of prayers we can pray because it is one the Lord has explicitly promised to answer (Lk. 11:5–13)!

Practising thankfulness

I think I've only met one Christian who regularly tells me that her prayer life is going well. The rest mumble and look at their shoes; even those who set time aside every day to pray can feel that they are losing the battle to be alert or earnest in their prayers. When hearing Paul's instruction to 'devote yourselves to prayer, being watchful and thankful' (Col. 4:2) so many of us know that faint, familiar guilt rising up. We perhaps send up a few more arrow prayers through the course of the day, but still feel stuck in prayerlessness.

There's help for us here, though, in the second part of that command. Gratitude and alertness can be the starter motor of prayer when new resolutions and lingering guilt fail. Perhaps the thought of being thankful sounds good in theory but impossible in practice. It's hard to see God's goodness when you're exhausted, feeling put-upon or your hormones leave you prone to cry over the smallest thing. We wonder what there is to feel thankful for. But pause and consider how Christ serves you every day.

Look to your world: the breath you breathe, the shelter over your head, the food on your plate, are all his gifts.

Look up and see the sky with its ever-changing light, and the trees on your way to work. He has made everything beautiful in its time, we only need to notice.

Look to the people around you. Consider the small acts of kindness and the wonderful variety of faces and frames: these are all glimpses of the image of God.

Then look to Jesus: he is the great physician, the shepherd of his sheep, the Lamb who was slain, the light in our darkness, the provider of spiritual water and food which satisfies and does not run out. He justifies and glorifies and even intercedes for us, day in, day out.

When we look at the world through the claims of scripture, seeing God as creator, sustainer, ruler and redeemer, we can't help but give thanks. And starting to pray prayers of thankfulness for all that he has done and is doing for us right now can be like fanning a dying fire. It will spark a flame of faith where there were only glowing embers because it teaches us who we are and who God is. We are desperately needy sinners; he is a generous, kind and just Father. This is the simplicity of vision George Herbert prays for. And though these are simple truths, they can lead into unexpected and important actions.

Age of ambition

The Guardian newspaper runs a regular column about changes people make in later midlife. We hear about divorces and PhDs; new businesses and travelling; skateboarding and sourdough. The contributors all reckoned that life was short and so they decided to do something different.

Pause

Sam Walker, a 50-year-old broadcaster, experienced a terrible perimenopause and decided to run the London Marathon as a means of getting her life back in shape. She sums up this outlook simply: 'don't sacrifice yourself for other people – do things for yourself'.[2] We women, the theories say, are socialised to be too nice to other people all the time. Instead, we owe it to ourselves to put self first.

It's a tempting message but one which runs in the opposite direction from the truth of God's Word. It might also seem totally impractical. Right now, you might be feeling up to your ears in demands: perimenopause or menopause, work and family have all piled the pressure on, and you can hardly see into next week, never mind the next decade. Putting myself first, you might think, fat chance! But a day is coming when you will be out of this phase of life; it may even be dawning very soon.

The bleeding will stop, night sweats will ease, your brain fog will lift. If you've children at home, they may well move out or at least grow in independence. Without those pressures, work may feel more contained. The great thing about travelling through and beyond menopause for many women, is that beyond this intermediate stage, lies a new era of life which God has designed for his purpose – a stage unencumbered by periods and childbearing.

What's more, by his common grace, the improvements of medical science have extended this stretch between the ending of our fertile years and the beginning of old age. The secular message, then, of 'do new things', and 'life

86

begins at ... [fill in the age!]' is not altogether wrong. We may well be looking at new opportunities and freedoms in our very near future.

The temptation, of course, is to buy into the me-first message: we end up wanting to 'do new things' for ourselves. Perhaps most of us don't dare state things so baldly, but in effect, this is the hope we're fixed on, the thing we're most looking forward to. Like Sam Walker, we may secretly be feeling: 'I've sacrificed myself for years; it will be my turn soon, time to do something for myself!' We're waiting for children to leave home, or to have built up our savings, or for retirement to get close, or the mortgage to be paid off, and then we'll get to do all those things we've dreamed of. Life will be easy and we can take it easy, whether that means booking an expensive holiday or drawing family close and shutting the front door to the world.

Such secret ambitions for comfort and ease don't fit with what God has in store for us, however. We have a better hope for the future: 'the hope of glory' (Col. 1:27). Inheritance, reward and future glory are ahead; life with Christ in a perfected world is the certain destination. And this solid hope for the future fills life now; we don't just have to dream.

The long-term hope of being with him should shape your short-term hopes in the next few years and decades. That means, now's a good time to pause and ask yourself, what do you hope he can do in and through you as you hit the heart of middle age? Do you have spiritual desires and ambitions?

Remember Katie, and the way she rediscovered the beauty of God's Word at the lowest point of her menopause experience? Today, Katie has left her English village for a training college, swapping the house she has lived in all her married life for a student room. Now post-menopause, the migraines have pretty much stopped and she's getting ready to serve overseas in Bible translation. Her husband is nearing retirement age and together they've decided that this is how they want to spend the next twelve years.

Katie's plan to take on a new and hard kind of work in a different continent isn't about chasing a long-held personal dream or an attempt to hold back the tide of inevitable ageing. Instead, she's pursuing an ambition the Lord has kindled in her own heart to seize an opportunity to serve.

Acting now

But opportunities aren't just for those who are married, or ready to travel, or good at languages. Colossians 4:5 tells us all to 'make the most of every opportunity' as we interact with non-Christians. The verb Paul uses here can often mean 'buy up'. Buying up the chances we get to share the good news of Christ isn't just about waiting for someone to ask us what we believe, but about deliberately spending our time, possibly our money and certainly our efforts to enable others to encounter Christ.

It's worth pausing and praying over the gifts and circumstances God has given you to reach out to others. It might involve inviting neighbours round, baking for an evangelistic event at church, helping in the youth group or sharing your church's posts online. It might be inviting someone to read one of the Gospels with you or giving wise advice to a non-Christian friend who's struggling and offering to pray for her. Buying up opportunities is active and costly. We absolutely need wisdom as we act and we need grace, understanding and clarity as we speak, but foremost we need a desire to 'buy' those costly opportunities, fuelled by our knowledge that the time is short and kindled by devoted prayer (Col. 4:2–6).

Katie's not on her own in embracing new opportunities post-menopause. Perhaps, like me, you know of women who have started fostering children, or of others who have begun teaching English to asylum seekers, or some who have taken on a paid role at church. And there have been many Katies through church history, too.

When I started researching women in the eighteenth and nineteenth centuries who served God, I was excited to discover those who, in their 40s and 50s and 60s, had a new lease of life. Children had grown up, they were more financially free, some had been widowed, or suffered other bereavement, and all had a new post-menopausal confidence about who they were. They had chosen to go far afield to share the gospel, or set up a school, or write a book, or start campaigning against injustice, or set up a local initiative to care for the needy.

And the same is true in the Bible. Think about the women whose stories have been saved for us: Naomi, for example, was a middle-aged woman whom God used to bring Ruth, the stranger who would become King David's grandmother, to trust in God. I wonder too, if some of Paul's female co-workers came from this age-bracket: maybe Priscilla, Phoebe and Lydia who hosted churches, taught the gospel and laboured alongside the apostles, did so in part because of the new freedom being in midlife brought. Though society has always told its 'mother-in-law' jokes, and has a tendency to write off the 'old hags' who are over the hill, the Lord is in the business of using middle-aged women to progress his kingdom all over the world, because he loves using the supposedly weak things to shame the strong.

You may not see yourself as a great initiator, and the changes you can make might seem small. Still, consider where you are and the many avenues the Lord has already given you to share his love. How might these expand as you head through the next decade? In our local communities, middle-aged women are active, and we can join them. Whether it is a choir, gym, book group, or food bank, you'll find women gathering. Joining a group and then doing the slow work of building friendships, sharing the details of your life and asking questions about the lives of others, may seem a small thing, but is a way of buying up opportunities to speak words of life.

Speaking up

When I was a young mum, I had two heroines in my local church. They couldn't have been more different. One was a single lady in her 50s who had health problems but managed to work just about full time. Another was a widowed ex-missionary in her early 60s. One of these was tough and ready to challenge, the other was tender-hearted and always ready to listen. Both were hospitable and active in sharing their lives with others. Both radiated the love of Jesus: they loved to learn about him and were often talking about him to me and other younger women in church, as well as giving us practical help. I treasure their memories, and now I'm getting towards their age, I have to ask myself: Am I ready to do the same for women younger than me?

In Colossians 3, Paul sets out a vision of local church life in which 'the message of Christ dwell[s] among you richly, as you teach and admonish one another with all wisdom' (Col. 3:16). Older women are definitely part of that work. Likewise, its common today to hear teaching from Titus 2:3–5, where Paul urges Titus to 'teach the older women' not only to live godly lives, but also 'to teach what is good'.

It's fantastic that we're now seeing an emphasis on training women in many church settings; elders should be taking an active role in preparing middle-aged women for Bible teaching ministry. We must remember, though, that this 'teaching' isn't limited to Bible studies or giving talks, but is about the sharing of godly wisdom in all kinds of contexts.

We can teach what is good when we're chatting over coffee or popping round to help out a friend. We see this clearly as Paul lays out his purpose for elders to invest in training women. The older women need to be equipped to 'urge the younger women to love their husbands and children, to be self-controlled and pure, to be busy at home, to be kind, and to be subject to their husbands, so that no one will malign the word of God' (Tit. 2:4–5).

In this way, Christian women are to be like killer whales. You may be surprised, but consider this: killer whales are one of only six species in which females live beyond their fertile years in the wild, and scientists think a reason for this is the significant role these older animals play in their groups. Professor Darren Croft says, 'Just as in humans, it seems that older female whales play a vital role in their societies – using their knowledge and experience to provide benefits including finding food and resolving conflict.'[3] We don't need to be evolutionary biologists to agree with this understanding of our social purpose. If life experience helps mature whales bring peace and comfort to their communities, how much more can we!

Middle-aged women are uniquely placed to help younger women live their lives in a godly way – whether or not they are married or have children. And to do this well, they need to be direct and clear. This is exactly what Paul is talking about when he urges the Colossians to teach and admonish one another 'with all wisdom'; it is only by doing this that the Word of Christ can live among us 'richly', uniting us, and giving us peace (Col. 3:16).

Perhaps this kind of teaching and training sounds bossy or interfering. It might be tempting to think that those in their 20s and 30s don't want to hear what you've got to say. And if all you're going to say begins with 'Back in the day', then maybe your assumption is right. But I know that when I was 25, I was as hungry to hear the advice and insights of older women as I was to receive their well-cooked food. I was sad that so many hung back. I wanted to know their wisdom on how to trust God when it was hard; I wanted to hear their stories of his faithfulness and their insights into his Word, and I even wanted them to tell me (gently, of course) when I was getting it wrong.

Whatever you do

Our work and our families take up time. And it's good to be working hard in a secular job or project if our hearts are fixed on Christ; it's no accident that Paul tells the Colossians twice in quick succession that whatever they do they should do it for the Lord Jesus (Col. 3:17, 23). We can't all head off to new fields of service like Katie, or even take up significant new duties where we are, but we can invest in the churches where God has placed us, doing that 'whatever' he has given us to do.

That might well not mean doing more. It could even mean doing fewer things better, with a clearer ambition to serve Christ well. You can look out for younger women, particularly, as well as others in our church families, and offer them, not only practical care, but also words which help them walk with God. You can be a friend or neighbour who prays for and seeks opportunities to speak of Christ.

Whether or not you have biological children, you can be (as Deborah is called in Judges 5:7) 'a mother in Israel', one whose words are wise and whose actions nurture others.

Reflection:

1. Are there any ways in which you are going through the motions or are cynical in your Christian service?

2. In what ways would you like to serve, whether now or in the future? Is there one younger woman at church you could draw alongside, or are there opportunities in your local area for developing better friendships with non-Christians?

3. Spend some time praying, either on your own or with a trusted friend, about this simple vision of faith. Can you commit to praying regular prayers of thanksgiving and confession of need? And can you pray for each other, in this battle to live simply fixed on Christ?

Conclusion

※　　　※　　　※

Why This Is Not the End

※　　　※　　　※

It's been a few years since that I'm-turning-into-my-mother shock in front of the mirror. Since then I've continued to age, of course. I've got more grey hairs and no doubt my wrinkles have deepened. And, just as I was learning not to pay them too much attention, my hot flushes became less frequent and my sleep improved. The difficult menopausal symptoms are reducing, and new horizons have opened.

What seemed monumental at the time, this movement from menstruation to menopause, has nearly passed, and what seemed so permanent, having the noise of children filling the house, has vanished.

My youngest child is now only living at home part-time; he's beginning to fledge as his siblings have done. Sadly, my father-in-law has had a stroke and moved into a care home. I continue to teach English, having navigated past those scary brain-fog blocks, and I've had increasing opportunities to speak and write.

Like Katie in our previous chapter, I'm looking out, asking the question, what could be next? There might be exciting new projects or there could be just more of the same. Parents will certainly need more help over the coming years, not less, and my big children will still call with their questions and requests for support. But whatever is ahead, it won't be for ever.

Time slips by, and each of life's phases is just a short step along the way. As one of Shakespeare's characters observed:

All the world's a stage
And all the men and women merely players;
They have their exits and their entrances;
And one man in his time plays many parts ...[1]

In Psalm 103, David agrees with this sense of brevity. Mortals are 'like grass, they flourish like a flower of the field; the wind blows over it and it is gone, and its place remembers it no more' (Ps. 103:15–16). We are dusty and frail. But whereas in Shakespeare this is a cause for humour, as we see the 'puking and mewling infant' quickly become the 'lean and slipper'd' old man, for David it's an opportunity to sing God's praises.

In the psalm, the truth of our frailty only highlights the wonder of God's love. David preaches to himself, 'Praise the LORD, my soul, and forget not all his benefits' (Ps. 103:2). His love is 'with those who fear him' 'from everlasting to everlasting' (Ps. 103:17). He has compassion, healing and forgiving (Ps. 103:3). We must make all effort to remember this truth as the days move on: our mortal flesh decays, his kindness remains.

And there's more that David wants to hold on to. The Lord's eternal love means that the 'youth' of those who fear him, 'is renewed like the eagle's' (Ps. 103:5). We middle-aged women feel our dustiness keenly; our lives can feel very frail. But the Lord is our renewer; he brings everlasting life through Christ's death, and he refreshes us again, and again, and again on the way to that eternal rest.

The way the Lord carries out this renewal work is surprising. It isn't by some supernatural infusion of physical power, as in a superhero movie. It's not through an exercise or dietary regime, or even increased rest, though these can all be of use. The prime way the Lord refreshes is he 'satisfies your desires with good things' (Ps. 103:5). These good things – love, compassion, forgiveness and grace – are all inseparable from God's own self. If we want to be renewed, we must want him. His love will be more than enough to quench all our thirst for comfort and rest and significance.

And this is our ultimate calling. There are abundant opportunities to serve those around us, but we meet these needs best by being satisfied by the love of our Saviour, Christ. And even if we are locked into our homes by illness or family duties, we still serve through being satisfied in him.

Seventeenth-century poet John Milton lost his sight in midlife, and wrestling with his sense of uselessness, came to the conclusion that God doesn't need our work, as if he's somehow dependent on us. Instead, those trusting him whatever their situation 'serve him best'. While many are active for Christ, 'They also serve who only stand and wait.'[2]

By God's grace we can be like the eagles whose old, worn-out feathers drop only to be replaced by new plumage, so that we can keep on flying. Katie experienced renewal as she cried out to her Lord in the hard times of menopause, and I too can testify to the refreshing power of his loving kindness.

In midlife as we start to droop we can pray for a revival of simple trust, and a new closeness to the one who understands our struggles. He 'knows how we are formed [and] remembers that we are dust' and wonderfully 'crowns [us] with love and compassion' (Ps. 103:14, 4).

My story doesn't end here, and neither does yours. The years of ageing will give way to the time when we'll be completely transformed spiritually and physically too. In that day, our Lord will not just pause the decay and death of this life but stop them completely. As my years pass, I become more eager for our Saviour's return. May midlife and menopause stir up in us all the prayer, 'Come Lord Jesus!'

Acknowledgments

* * *

First thanks go to Lewis and my children who have borne with me through the writing process, over holidays, in evenings and at weekends. I'm so grateful for your patience and prayers. Thanks also to Natalie Brand and her online group of female writers whose apposite comments prompted me to turn an article-length piece into this book. Sheri Newton has been a fantastic editor; thanks for all your warmth, encouragement and your sharp eyes! Last, of course, all thanks, praise and glory to God who has proved his goodness to me in so many ways; he truly renews our youth like the eagle's!

Endnotes

Introduction

1. Premature menopause is described as one which comes before the age of 40. Ninety per cent of these do not have a known cause. Five per cent of women experience their periods stopping between the age of 40 and 45 and this is classed as 'early' natural menopause. For the rest, menopause hits between 45 and 55. See https://www.nhsinform.scot/ healthy-living/womens-health/later-years-around-50-years-and-over/ menopause-and-post-menopause-health/early-and-premature-menopause/. It's worth remembering that the level of symptoms experienced varies hugely. A worldwide 2021 survey quoted in the *British Medical Journal* judges that between 16 and 40 per cent of women will experience 'moderate to severe' symptoms – that's a wide range but still, thankfully, leaves the majority in the 'mild' category. See Martha Hickey, Myra S. Hunter, Nanette Santoro and Jane Ussher, 'Normalising Menopause', *British Medical Journal*, 15 June 2022, available at https:// www.bmj.com/content/bmj/377/bmj-2021-069369.full.pdf.

2. Sayeeda Warsi in Kaye Adams and Vicky Allan, *Still Hot! 42 Brilliantly Honest Menopause Stories* (Black & White Publishing, 2020), 10.

3. Mariella Frostrup and Alice Smellie, *Cracking the Menopause: While Keeping Yourself Together* (Bluebird, 2021).

4. Davina McCall and Naomi Potter, *Menopausing: The Positive Roadmap to Your Second Spring* (HQ, 2022), cover copy.

Chapter 1

1. From Virginia Woolf's short story, *The Mark on The Wall* (1917), available at https://www.online-literature.com/virginia_woolf/855/ (accessed 2/2/2024).

2. Dylan Thomas, 'Do Not Go Gentle into That Good Night' (1939), available at https://www.poetryfoundation.org/poems/46569/do-not-go-gentle-into-that-good-night (accessed 1/1/2024).

Chapter 2

1. There's an important caveat to this point. It might be that you are struggling with destructive habits or are in a situation of abuse, and in these cases, 'moving on' is necessary but will require significant support. Sometimes it is only when we are away from a dangerous and difficult situation that we can properly understand it. Do seek help from a trusted Christian friend and professional agencies.

Endnotes

2. Timothy Keller, *The Meaning of Marriage: Facing the Complexities of Commitment with the Wisdom of God* (Hodder and Stoughton, 2011), 44.

3. Paul David Tripp, *Lost in the Middle: Midlife Crisis and the Grace of God* (Shepherd's Press, 2009), 33.

Chapter 3

1. Kimberly Ann Yonkers, Shaughn O'Brien and Elias Eriksson, 'Premenstrual Syndrome', *The Lancet*, 05 April 2008, available at https://www.thelancet.com/journals/lancet/article/PIIS0140-6736(08)60527-9/fulltext (accessed 2/2/2024).

2. It is reckoned that about 90 per cent of women experience some degree of disrupted feelings (along with some physical discomfort), in the days running up to their period and, for between 5 and 8 per cent of women, these symptoms are very severe, affecting their lives in a significant way. See Martha Hickey, Myra S. Hunter, Nanette Santoro and Jane Ussher, 'Normalising Menopause', *British Medical Journal*, 15 June 2022, available at https://www.bmj.com/content/bmj/377/bmj-2021-069369.full.pdf.

3. Kaye Adams and Vicky Allan, *Still Hot! 42 Brilliantly Honest Menopause Stories* (Black & White Publishing, 2020), 52.

4. Ibid., 57.

5. Keri Folmar, 'On Seasons of Hormonal Change', *Priscilla Talk*, Episode 20.

6. See Carl Baker and Esme Kirk-Wade, 'Mental Health Statistics', *House of Commons Library*, 13 March 2023, available at https://researchbriefings.files.parliament.uk/documents/SN06988/SN06988.pdf.

7. Martin Luther, *Commentary on Romans*, translated by J. Theodore Mueller (Zondervan, 1954), 91.

8. Thomas Goodwin, *The Heart of Christ* (Banner of Truth, 2011), 156.

9. Brother Lawrence, *The Practice of the Presence of God*, Second Letter, available at https://ccel.org/ccel/lawrence/practice/practice.iv.ii.html (accessed 24/1/2024).

10. Joe Barnard, *Hymn Workouts: 100 Exercises to Set Your Heart Ablaze* (Christian Focus Publications, 2022).

Chapter 4

1. Mariella Frostrup and Alice Smellie, *Cracking the Menopause: While Keeping Yourself Together* (Bluebird, 2021), 192.

2. Quoted in Helen Dennis, 'How Older Women Can Combat Feeling Invisible or Unseen in Social Situations', *Los Angeles Daily News*, 24 July 2022, available at https://www.dailynews.com/2022/07/24/how-older-women-can-combat-feeling-invisible-or-unseen-in-social-situations/.

3. Virginia Woolf, *Mrs Dalloway* (Penguin, 1925), 8.

4. Manohla Dargis, 'Review: "Hello, My Name Is Doris," About an Older Woman's Love for a Much Younger Man', *New York Times*, 10 March 2016, available at https://www.nytimes.com/2016/03/11/movies/sally-field-hello-my-name-is-doris-review.html.

5. Bo Helmich, 'Theology and Beauty; An Enquiry', in *Modern Reformation*, 1 May 2021, available at https://modernreformation.org/resource-library/essays/theology-and-beauty-an-enquiry/.

6. Kathleen Stott, 'Kylie Minogue's Glorious Artifice', *Unherd*, 26 May 2023, available at https://unherd.com/2023/05/kylie-minogues-glorious-artifice/.

7. C.S. Lewis, *The Weight of Glory* (1941), 6, available at https://www.wheelersburg.net/Downloads/Lewis%20Glory.pdf (accessed 23/8/23).

8. Ibid.

9. Thanks to David Dent!

10. William Hendriksen, *New Testament Commentary: Colossians* (Banner of Truth, 1971), 150.

11. The verb contemplate can also be translated 'reflect', but of course, to reflect implies contemplation, for a mirror only reflects the person looking in it.

Chapter 5

1. This data is broken down here: 'Analysis of Sandwich Caring, United Kingdom', *Office for National Statistics*, 14 January 2019, available at: https://www.ons.gov.uk/peoplepopulationandcommunity/healthandsocialcare/healthandwellbeing/datasets/sandwichcarers.

2. Ibid.

3. Jenny Éclair, *Older and Wider* (Quercus, 2021), 209.

4. N.T. Wright, *Colossians and Philemon*, Tyndale New Testament Commentaries (IVP, 1987), 145.

5. Ann Benton, *If It's Not Too Much Trouble: The Challenge of the Aged Parent* (Christian Focus, 2016), 14.

6. Ibid., 31.

7. Andrew and Rachel Wilson, *The Life You Never Expected: Thriving while Parenting Special Needs Children* (IVP, 2015), 25.

8. Loss of libido is common during menopause and may be due to hormonal factors and compounded by emotional strain and change as well. It may well return after menopause. The reduction in oestrogen results in vaginal dryness and lack of elasticity which can make intercourse uncomfortable. All of these can place strain on a marital relationship, but there are plenty of natural remedies: use of lubrication; paying attention to building the intimacy of your relationship in other

ways; pelvic floor exercises; and not giving up on intercourse (the less sex you have, the harder it will be!). Also available are oestrogen gels and pessaries which directly target the vagina and do not have the side effects of other forms of HRT.

9. J.C. Ryle, *Living or Dead? A Series of Home Truths* (Robert Carter & Brothers, 1851), 262–265.

10. Ann Benton, *If It's Not Too Much Trouble: The Challenge of the Aged Parent* (Christian Focus, 2016), 98–99.

Chapter 6

1. George Herbert, 'A Wreath' (1633), available at https://www.ccel. org/h/herbert/temple/Wreath.html (accessed 26/1/2024).

2. Sam Walker, 'Running Up That Hill' *Effin Hormones*, Season 3, Episode 7.

3. 'Male Killer Whales Protected by Post-menopause Mums', *University of York*, 20 July 2023, available at https://www.york.ac.uk/ news-and-events/news/2023/research/male-whales-protected-by-post-menopause-mums/#:~:text=Only%20six%20species%20 %E2%80%93%20humans%20and,puzzled%20about%20why%20 this%20occurs. See also Hannah Devlin, 'Post-menopausal Killer Whales Defend their Sons from Aggressors, Study Finds', The Guardian, 20 July 2023, available at https://www.theguardian.com/ environment/2023/jul/20/post-menopausal-killer-whales-defend-sons-research-finds#:~:text=%E2%80%9CThe%20similarities%20 with%20humans%20are,finding%20food%20and%20resolving%20 conflict.%E2%80%9D.

Conclusion

1. Jaques in William Shakespeare, *As You Like It*, Act II Scene vii, available at https://www.poetryfoundation.org/poems/56966/speech-all-the-worlds-a-stage (accessed 30/1/2024).

2. John Milton, 'Sonnet 19: When I Consider How My Light Is Spent' (1655), available at https://www.poetryfoundation.org/poems/44750/ sonnet-19-when-i-consider-how-my-light-is-spent (accessed 31/1/2024).

More books from 10Publishing

Resources that point to Jesus